3/05

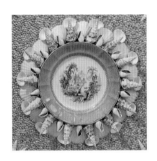

Beyond the Basics
MOSAICS

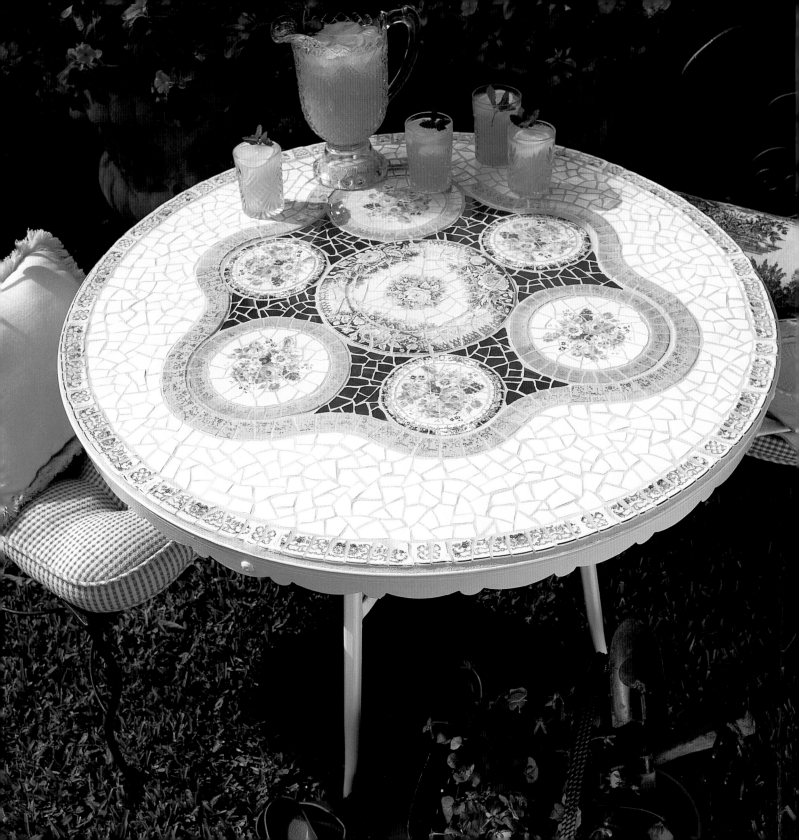

Beyond the Basics
MOSAICS

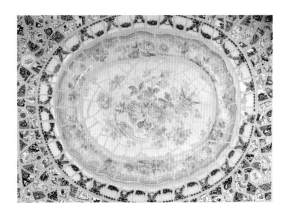

ELIZABETH DUVAL

STERLING PUBLISHING CO., INC. NEW YORK
A STERLING / CHAPELLE BOOK

CHAPELLE, LTD.

Jo Packham • Sara Toliver • Cindy Stoeckl

Editor: Leslie Farmer
Book Design: Renato Stanisic Design
Photography: Ryne Hazen for Hazen Photography
David Fowler for Talent Group, Inc.
Photo Stylists: Rebecca Ittner, Suzy Skadburg
Art Director: Karla Haberstich
Copy Editor: Marilyn Goff
Staff: Kelly Ashkettle, Areta Bingham, Anne Bruns, Donna Chambers,
Emily Frandsen, Lana Hall, Susan Jorgensen, Jennifer Luman,
Melissa Maynard, Barbara Milburn, Lecia Monsen,
Kim Taylor, Linda Venditti, Desirée Wybrow

Library of Congress Cataloging-in-Publication Data Available

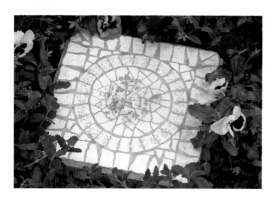

Every effort has been made to ensure that all information in this book is accurate. However, due to differing conditions, tools, and individual skills, the publisher cannot be responsible for any injuries, losses, and/or other damages which may result from the use of the information in this book.

If you have questions or comments, please contact:
Chapelle, Ltd., Inc.,
P.O. Box 9252, Ogden, UT 84409
(801) 621-2777 • (801) 621-2788 Fax
e-mail: chapelle@chapelleltd.com
Web site: chapelleltd.com

10 9 8 7 6 5 4 3 2 1

Published by Sterling Publishing Co., Inc.
387 Park Avenue South, New York, NY 10016
©2004 by Elizabeth DuVal
Distributed in Canada by Sterling Publishing
c/o Canadian Manda Group, One Atlantic Avenue, Suite 105
Toronto, Ontario, Canada M6K 3E7
Distributed in Great Britain by Chrysalis Books Group PLC,
The Chrysalis Building, Bramley Road, London W10 6SP, England
Distributed in Australia by Capricorn Link (Australia) Pty. Ltd.
P.O. Box 704, Windsor, NSW 2756, Australia
Printed in China
All Rights Reserved

Sterling ISBN 1-4027-0936-6

Space would not permit the inclusion of every decorating item photographed for this book, nor could all of the designers be identified. Many of these items may be referred to on the Ruby & Begonia Web site: www.rubyandbegonia.com or by calling (801) 334-7829.

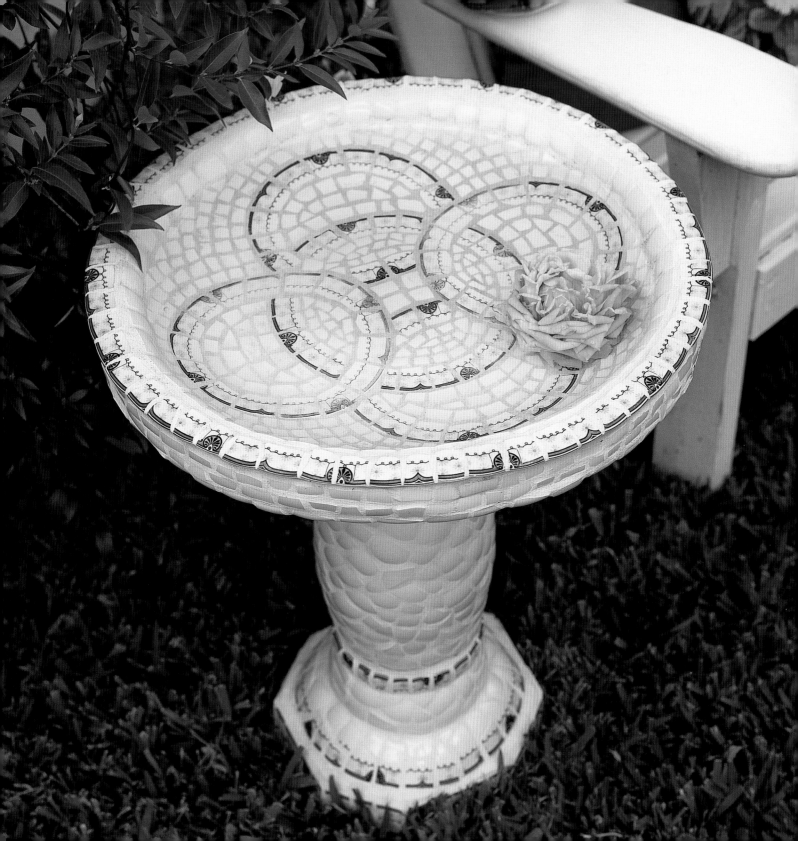

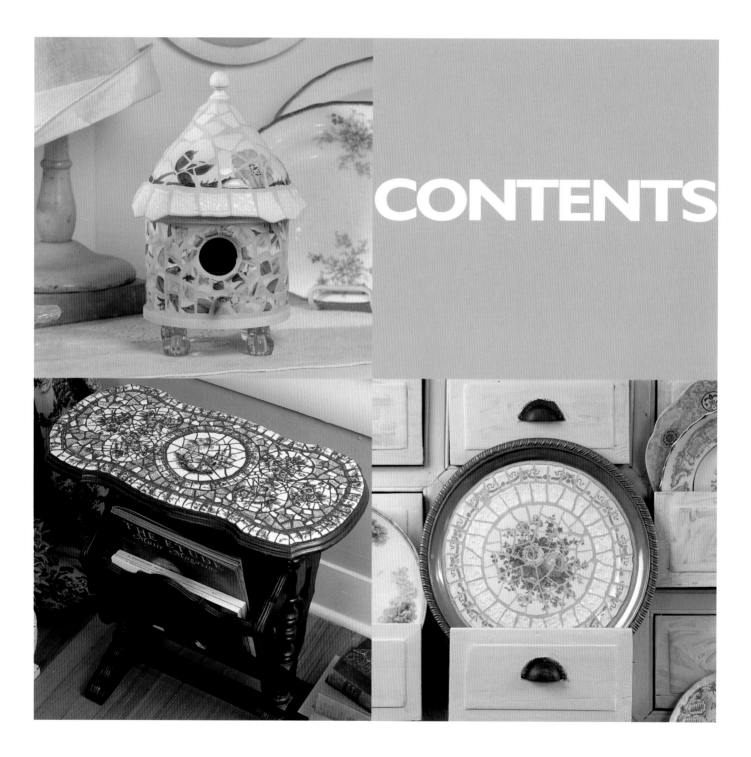

CONTENTS

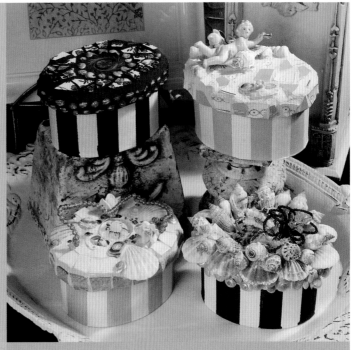

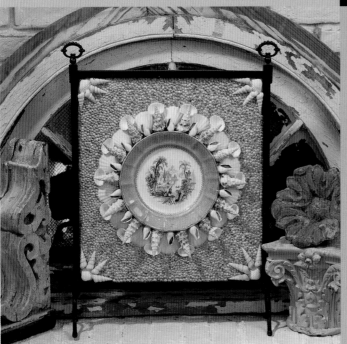

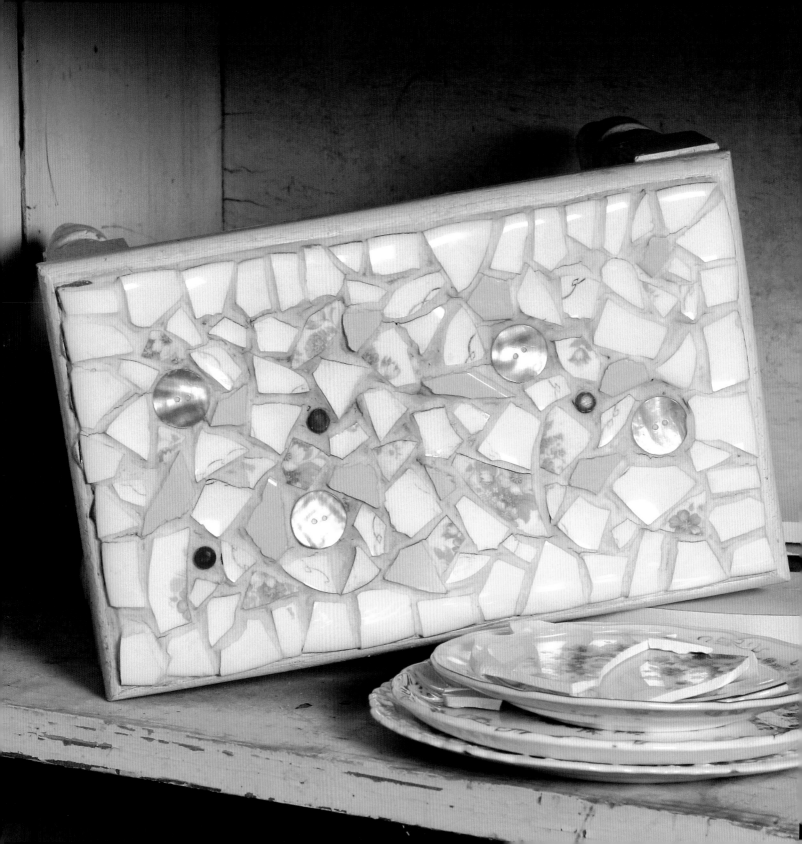

BELOW TOP: *The Picture Frame on pages 55–57 is displayed on an antique mirror with a string of crystals and an antique brooch.*

BELOW BOTTOM: *Tan china and grout complement a vintage sepia-toned photograph.*

INTRODUCTION

Mosaics have been around for centuries. They are such a wonderful art form because they are at home in almost any setting—from the most formal to the most casual. The best part about mosaics is that they require little training and can be enjoyed by anyone, even if you are on a budget.

I began my career as a mosaic designer literally hours after seeing a 10 minute segment on a home design TV show. It featured a New York artist who incorporated china plates into her mosaics. I was instantly intrigued and inspired. I was so excited I could hardly contain myself. It was perfect for me—I love old dishes, I love old furniture, and I love saving old discarded things and giving them a new and purposeful life. I jumped in my car and drove to my local hardware store. I rushed to the tile aisle. Enthusiastically, I explained to the gentleman there what a wonderful thing I had just seen on TV and that I had to get started right away. "What supplies do I need to cover a 5" x 7" footstool with bowls and buttons?" I asked. He stared blankly at me and, after a pause that lasted at least 20 seconds, he said, "You wanna do what?"

From that moment on, I decided to do it on my own. Luckily for me, chipped-china mosaics, or Picasiette, are not at all difficult. However, one of the risks you take when

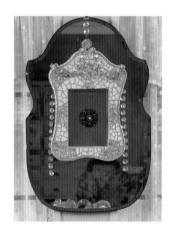

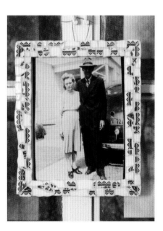

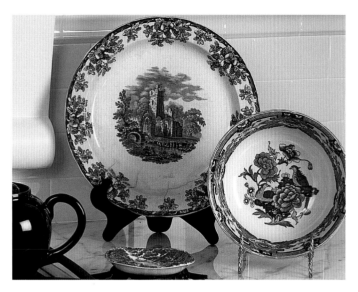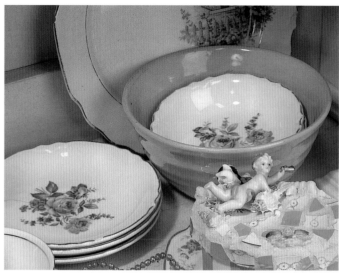

ABOVE LEFT: *It is relatively easy to find dishes of a similar color and pattern for use in a monochromatic mosaic.*

ABOVE RIGHT: *Try to maintain some organization in your collection of dishes. Keep similar colors and patterns together while in storage to ease the process of selecting materials for a particular mosaic design.*

getting involved with mosaics that use china and found objects is that once you start accumulating materials, you cannot stop—if the price is right and you can fit it in your car, you will take it home. You may not be certain what to do with it just yet, but you will not be able to pass it up because you know it is going to be just perfect on something.

I have many shelves full of dishes—entire sets of dishes, as well as orphaned spare dishes, bowls, platters, cups, saucers, creamers, sugar bowls, and salt and pepper shakers. Then there are the dish parts, which include sugar bowl lids, cup handles, and the always handy teapot spouts—you never know when you might want to add a bit of whimsy. Needless to say, clutter control can very quickly become an issue in your home or workspace.

Although I have never taken any classes and am not a formally trained artist, I have been successfully working as a mosaic artist for the last five years. I have not used traditional mosaic tiles in my pieces because I am much happier cutting the tesserae I need from a vintage plate rather than buying little pieces of mosaic tile at the art supply store. The closest I have come to using traditional tesserae is in adding an occasional spattering of stained glass in a project when I felt it needed a jolt of color. However, there is a whole world of gorgeous glass, ceramic, and natural stone tiles made specifically for use in mosaics. And there is no reason why you should not explore these as options for use in your projects.

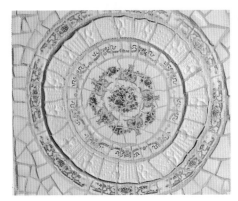
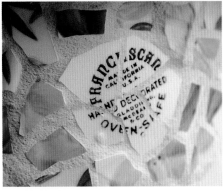
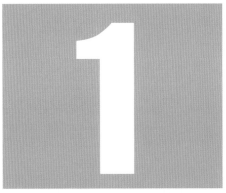
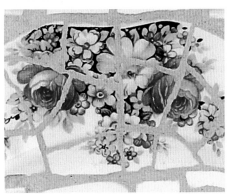
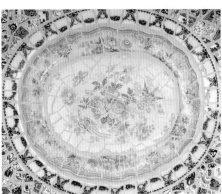

Picasiette

PICASIETTE, OR PIQUE-ASSIETTE, is a style of mosaic which uses pieces of broken ceramics (mainly plates, bowls, and cups) and other found objects in the design. The predominant medium for most picasiette pieces is china.

There are several definitions for the phrase pique-assiette. The name loosely translates as "stolen plate," "plate stealer," or "broken plate." The word "pique" can mean crazy. It was used in the 1930s by neighbors of a man named Raymond Isidore. Isidore, it seems, enhanced his entire property—both inside and out—with intricate and decorative mosaics crafted from salvaged shards and found items. Apparently, the neighbors were less than enthusiastic about his artistic expression. Today, however, tens of thousands of visitors

ABOVE: *At first glance, many picasiette mosaics appear to be made up of randomly placed china pieces. However, upon closer inspection it is clear that there is a definite method to breaking the dishes and a planned out design that leads the construction of the piece.*

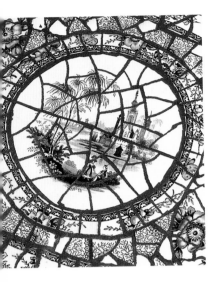

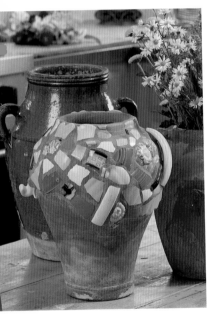

ABOVE: *The Magazine Stand on pages 86–87 is true to traditional picasiette form, while the Olive Oil Jug on pages 61–63 is a refined example of shard art.*

marvel at "La Maison Picasiette" in Chartres, northern France, and the term "pique-assiette" is used around the world.

It is unclear whether picasiette originated in France or was just named there. When I was in Paris on vacation, I inquired at every antique store; and most of the shopkeepers had examples of picasiette, but few knew any specifics regarding the history of the name. There was one shopkeeper who told me a charming story of how, many years ago, broken shards of china could easily be found along the beaches of coastal France. According to this Frenchman, trade ships often carried china as part of their cargo and when one of them wrecked, there was a lot of broken china to be found washed up on the beach. Women and children would collect the shards to take them home and create colorful mosaic projects. I have my suspicions as to the accuracy of this story, but it sounds good.

Mosaics that incorporate chipped china provide an avenue for artists to express their creativity in original and constructive ways, and at the same time preserve the past by recycling damaged and unwanted items. Just as certain scents can trigger vivid memories, fragments of objects or recognized patterns can evoke remembered associations with people, places, and events. Items with sentimental value, that have been packed away or that are not being used because they are slightly damaged, can be given a new lease on life. As you begin to incorporate these pieces into your artwork, you will find that they become very special to you and bring back cherished memories.

SHARD ART

Shard art is a more recent and currently very popular form of mosaic that tends to be less structured and not as intricate as traditional picasiette.

In shard art, anything goes. You can use old jewelry, buttons, keys, stones, marbles, coins, small figurines, etc., in your piece. You are limited only by your imagination—if you can get it to stick to your base's surface, you can include it in your mosaic.

If you want a more traditional mosaic design when working a piece using the shard art form, you must show a little restraint. While it is appropriate to use many different colors, textures, and materials in shard art pieces. Be careful because it can very easily become amateurish and cluttered.

SELECTING & ACQUIRING MATERIALS

Despite my initial experience with the footstool, one of the best pieces of advice I can give to someone who is trying picasiette for the first time is to go to the tile aisle at your local hardware store. There you will find practically everything you need to get started. If you have the patience to endure the look of disbelief on the store employee's face when you explain that you intend to use broken plates instead of tile to cover your backsplash, they can be a wealth of knowledge.

SELECTING CHINA

Scavenging for materials can be half the fun. Thrift stores, flea markets, antique shops, yard sales, and even your own basement or attic can turn up treasures. Make certain you let your friends and family know about your new passion. At first, you are likely to hear, "Oh! If only I'd known. I broke a beautiful teapot just last week, but I threw it out already." However, people will eventually start setting aside broken treasures to pass on to you, and before you know it, you will have boxes full of fabulous broken china ready to be turned into a fantastic work of art.

The first step to successfully breaking china is in selecting the right type of china. Not all china is suited for breaking, which is normally a good thing but not in the world of picasiette. The best types of china to look for are American and English pieces produced in the 1920s, '30s, and '40s. They are still plentiful and display wonderful floral designs. Names to look for are Taylor Smith Taylor, Homer Laughlin, Johnson Brothers, Pope Gosser, Steubenville, Knowles, KTK, Myott, and the list goes on. If the underside of the plate is a creamy off-white color, you know it will probably break cleanly.

Modern, or new, plates are very hard—almost like glass—and tend to shatter under the pressure of tile nippers, which are most often used for breaking (see Breaking with Tile Nippers on pages 15–19). If you have fallen in love with a specific pattern and must use it in your project, think about breaking the plate using the hammer method (see Breaking with a Hammer on pages 20–21), keeping in mind that you will not have a lot of control over your breaks. Most new china is marked on the back as dishwasher safe or microwave safe. Since microwaves did not exist in the '20s and '30s, the mark is a sure sign that you are

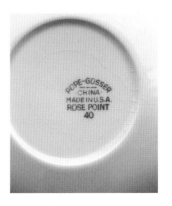

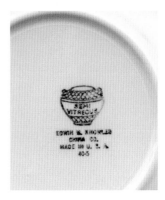

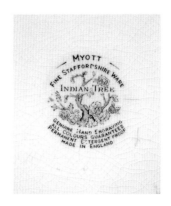

ABOVE: *Shown are three of the many maker's marks found on china that is suitable for picasiette mosaics.*

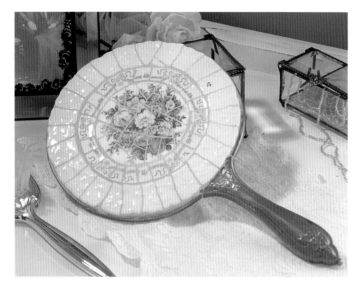

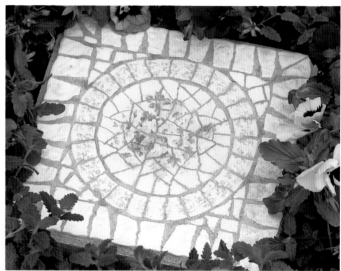

ABOVE LEFT: *The Hand Mirror on pages 50–51 is an excellent example of creating a mosaic on a metal-based surface.*

ABOVE RIGHT: *The Stepping Stone on pages 70–71 requires special selection of a base and materials that can stand up to outside weather conditions.*

looking at a modern piece of china. You will likely run into the same problem with real porcelain. If the underside of the plate is pure white, it is likely you are holding a piece of porcelain. Porcelain is also very hard and can be difficult to cut with tile nippers.

Another thing to be aware of is the shape and thickness of your china. Think about how smooth you want your finished piece to be. For example, if you are making a tabletop, you probably want to stick with flat plates and avoid the curved pieces that come from bowls and cups. Serving platters, although flat, are usually very thick and may cause unevenness in your design.

SELECTING A SURFACE, OR BASE

One of the most important steps in the mosaic process is selecting a surface that is appropriate for your project. Glass, metal, wood, and ceramic are ideal surfaces. It is crucial that you work on a rigid surface. If the surface is at all flexible, your china is likely to pop off, and your grout will crack.

Oftentimes, mosaic projects are required to be weatherproof. If you intend to place your finished item outside, I suggest that you use a product called gypsum board as your surface. Gypsum board is a concrete product designed to stand up to outside exposure without warping, molding, or decomposing. Gypsum board can be cut with a jigsaw; however, it is tough stuff, so do not expect to be using that saw blade again.

Gypsum board can be easily found at your local hardware store. Its only drawback is that it comes in 3' x 5' sheets. If the surface of your finished item needs to be wider than 3', cut a piece of treated plywood to the size you need, then use an outdoor construction adhesive to adhere the gypsum-board pieces over the plywood.

BREAKING

There are three methods for breaking china: 1) breaking with tile nippers; 2) breaking with a hammer; and 3) cutting with a wet saw. Deciding which method to use is not only a matter of preference but a matter of desired results in your finished project. Using the hammer allows for very little control over the size of the pieces or angle of the break. Using tile nippers allows you to achieve a more formal, structured design by maintaining the integrity of the plate's patterns. Nippers allow you to cut pieces to specific sizes for your designs. With practice, you can control the line of the cut, although you should not expect to achieve 100% accuracy. For that, you need a wet saw. If you choose to use a wet saw, be prepared to get wet.

Safety glasses are an absolute must when it comes to breaking china and tile. Chips fly off at high speeds over surprising distances; and if one gets in your eye, you will regret not having used the safety glasses. I can personally attest to that. It is also a good idea to keep bandages and fresh water nearby in case you cut yourself. You are dealing with sharp tessera edges and even sharper tile nippers.

BREAKING WITH TILE NIPPERS

The goal is to cut away the section that separates the plate center from the border. Keep in mind that you will have to overcome two obstacles—slope and ridge.

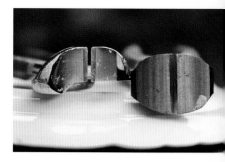

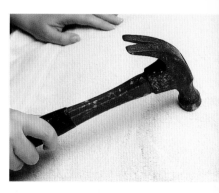

ABOVE: *Tile nippers and a hammer are the two most-used tools for breaking china for mosaics.*

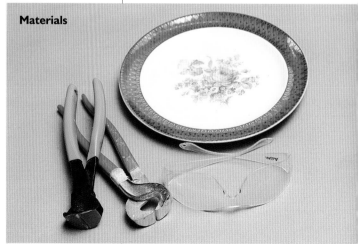

Materials

Materials needed to break with tile nippers:

• China: large dinner plate
• Tile nippers
• Safety glasses

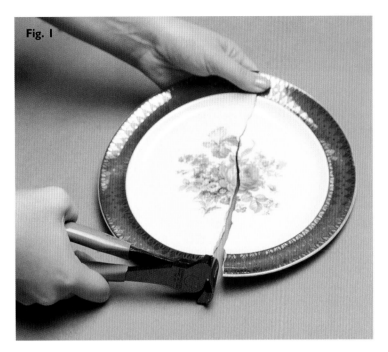

Fig. 1

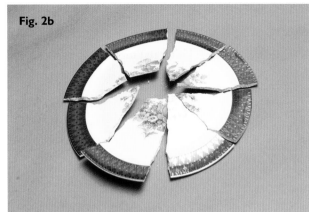

Fig. 2b

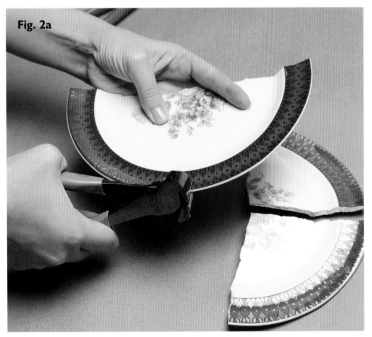

Fig. 2a

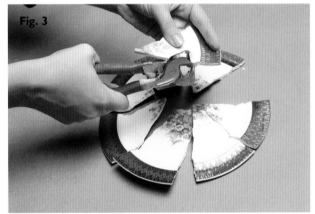

Fig. 3

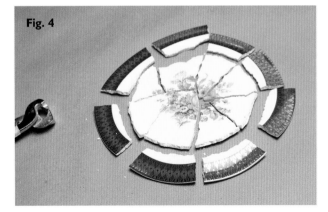

Fig. 4

INSTRUCTIONS

STEP 1

Put on safety glasses. Using the nippers, break the plate in half. (Fig. 1)

STEP 2

Break each half into quarters, then break each quarter into eighths. (Figs. 2a–2b)

STEP 3

Begin to separate the plate's border from its center. Pick up each piece and cut away the curved portion between border and center. Repeat this process for each section. Try to keep pieces in order. (Fig. 3)

STEP 4

Now the plate is separated into two usable components, the central design and a border. However, it still needs to be flattened out in order to be applied to the surface. (Fig. 4)

STEP 5

Concentrating on one section at a time, start on the border by cutting each piece. Pick up each piece and place the outside edge just ¼" or so inside the mouth of the nippers. Hold the piece in your least dominant hand across from the nippers. Make certain that the angle of the nippers reflects where you want the cut to be. Breaking each section into three or four pieces works best. (Fig. 5)

STEP 6

These pieces are still rough and not very flat; the little tail that is left must be cut away from the slope of the plate. To do this, find the point where the border dips down into the slope and place your nippers at this point. Again, catch only the outside ¼" with the nippers. If you start the cut precisely at the edge of that bend, you will usually get a clean cut across. Squeeze down and it should break cleanly along this line. You may have to do the same thing on the opposite side as well. This should result in a flat wedge. (Fig. 6)

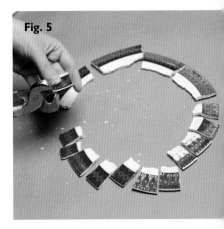

Fig. 5

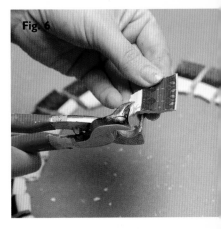

Fig. 6

Tip:

Experiment with the angle at which you hold the tile nippers to the china piece. You will see that this often determines the outcome of the cut more than you might think. Try to be consistent when making cuts on pieces that will be placed near each other on the mosaic project.

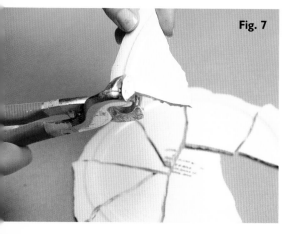

Fig. 7

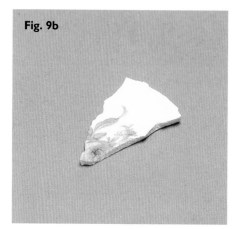

Fig. 9b

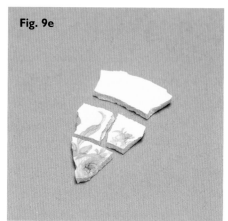

Fig. 9e

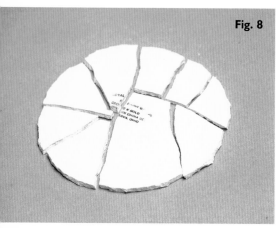

Fig. 8

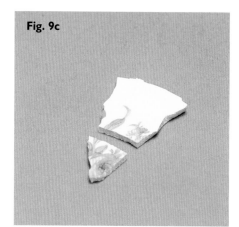

Fig. 9c

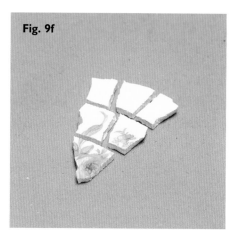

Fig. 9f

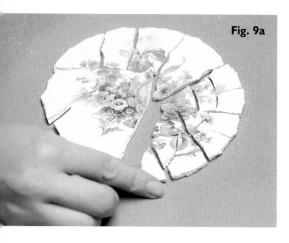

Fig. 9a

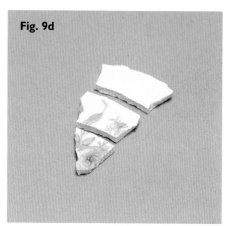

Fig. 9d

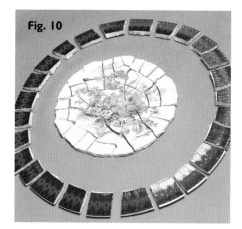

Fig. 10

STEP 7

Start on the center section by removing the ridge at the back of the plate. Place the nippers as close to the ridge as possible and nip away a little bit at a time. Remember to use only the very edge of the nipper. You may have to make two or three attempts from each side until the ridge is removed entirely. Repeat on all pieces and keep them in order. (Fig. 7)

STEP 8

Now you have a flat central design, but it still must be broken into smaller pieces before it is ready to be applied to the mosaic. (Fig. 8)

STEP 9

It is very important to break up the pieces in a uniform fashion that allows for regular spacing between each piece when you put the pattern back together. To do this, it helps to look at each triangular section as a piece of pie, and the cuts as bites of that piece of pie. The first bite will be at the very tip; just one bite will be enough. You are left with a wider section to bite from now. It will probably take two bites to get across the front edge of the pie wedge. As you move toward the "crust" section, you will have to take three or four bites to finish it all. Continue cutting each piece. By cutting more pieces at the back edge and fewer pieces at the front tip, you allow the wedge to grow in proportion to its original shape. Therefore, when you put it back together you will have a circle, rather than an oval. (Figs. 9a–9f)

STEP 10

You now have both a border and central design that are flat and ready to apply onto the base surface. (Fig. 10)

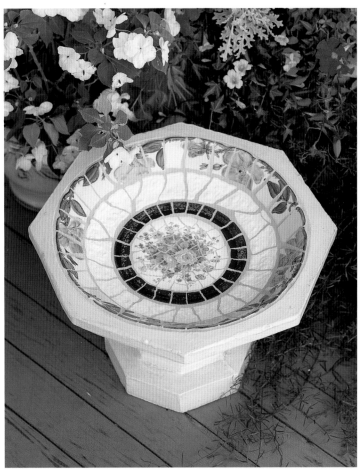

ABOVE: *The circular design of the English-style Birdbath on pages 72–73 incorporates a dish with a distinct outside border and uses the Breaking with Tile Nippers technique shown here.*

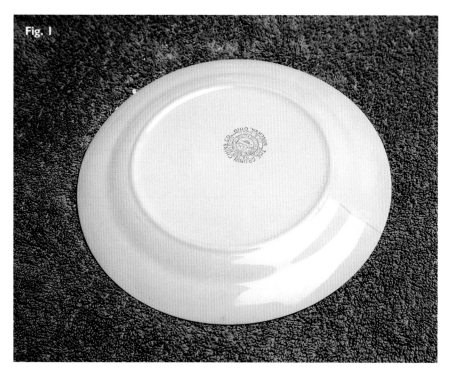

Fig. 1

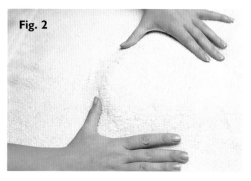

Fig. 2

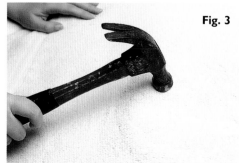

Fig. 3

BREAKING WITH A HAMMER

INSTRUCTIONS

STEP 1

Place one or two folded terry cloth bath towels on concrete or other hard surface so you have two to four thicknesses of toweling. Place the plate upside down on the towels. (Fig. 1)

STEP 2

Place one towel over the top of the plate to keep chips from flying out. Use your hands to feel through the towel and locate where the ridge is on the bottom of the plate. (Fig. 2)

STEP 3

Put on the safety glasses. Imagine that the ridge on the back of the plate is a clock face, then use the hammer to hit the ridge at 12, 3, 6, and 9 o'clock to break the plate into manageable pieces. Avoid beginning the break by hitting the plate in the center as you will

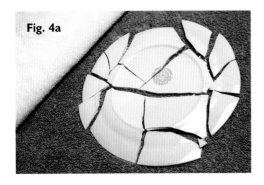

Fig. 4a

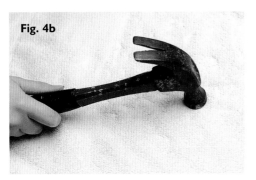

Fig. 4b

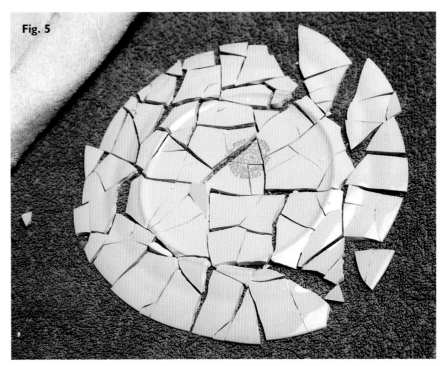

Fig. 5

oftentimes end up with a large hole in the middle of the plate and a plate border that is fully intact. Also avoid beginning the break by hitting the plate edge as you are likely to shatter the border or chip the plate. (Fig. 3)

STEP 4

Lift the top towel up periodically to see how the breaks are progressing. You may decide to stop using a hammer and begin using nippers to "clean up" the pieces, or you may want to continue breaking with the hammer. It really depends on the type and size of shards the project requires. (Figs. 4a–4b)

STEP 5

If you choose to continue with a hammer, always keep the plate covered with the top towel. Continue hitting the plate all over until the desired size pieces are achieved. Try to keep them in order as you move them to your picasiette project. (Fig. 5)

Tips:

Try to keep your pieces in order on the toweling. You may want to slide a board underneath the toweling and use it to transport the pieces to your work area.

Since china will not break predictably, do not get too upset if the breaks are not as you had envisioned. Be flexible when working with the broken pieces and let them guide you to placing them on the piece. It likely will turn out better than you had originally imagined.

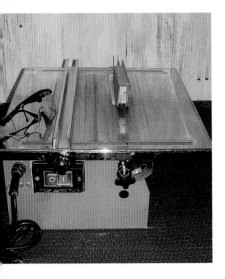

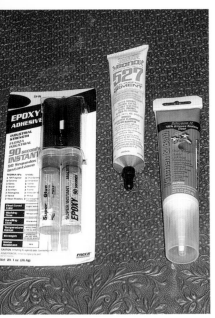

CUTTING WITH A WET SAW

The wet saw works well if you want to cut straight lines or if you have a piece of china that simply is not breaking well with nippers and you do not want to use the hammer method on it. On the few occasions that I have had to use a hard porcelain piece in my design, I have found that the wet saw helps me control the cuts, especially around the outside border.

Wet saws are not as dangerous as traditional wood-cutting saws, but you should use extreme caution when cutting plates with one of them. Wet saws are actually designed to cut flat tile, not curved uneven dishes. Therefore, you sometimes must hold the dishes at odd angles in order to get the results you want and are often unable to use the cutting-blade guard. The biggest danger is not so much that of cutting yourself as it is of getting slivers of china in your eyes. You must at least wear safety glasses, and I strongly recommend investing in a face shield. You also may want to put on a raincoat because the spray from the water will be hitting you right in the chest.

Follow the manufacturer's instructions for the saw you are using. Keep an extra-close eye on the water level. When the blade guard is in use, it helps direct the water flow back into the reservoir. However, if you must raise or remove the guard, the water tends to spray out of the machine and cannot flow back into the reservoir.

ADHESIVES & ACCESSORIES

There are several different types of adhesives that can be used for attaching tesserae onto a base. Each has its own set of characteristics that determines how and where it can best be applied. Make certain to use the correct type of adhesive to complement each surface and the intended use of your mosaic.

Bond 527—Bond 527 is a very strong, clear all-purpose adhesive. It is fast drying and flexible once dry. Bond 527 can be used on most surfaces including china, wood, glass, metal, and plastics.

Clear Silicone—Clear silicone is great for projects worked on glass or for anytime you are worried about seeing the adhesive. Silicone can be purchased in small handheld tubes or large tubes designed to be used with ratchet guns. The small tubes are much more convenient but a lot more expensive than the large tubes.

ABOVE TOP: *Shown is a wet saw for cutting tile.*

ABOVE BOTTOM: *Shown are epoxy, Bond 527, and clear silicone adhesives.*

Epoxy—When all else fails, use epoxy. It can be used on a piece that will be placed indoors or outdoors. You should be able to find a type of epoxy that will adhere to practically anything. Epoxy is a good choice for old jewelry, three-dimensional, or heavy objects. You can usually find a clear epoxy so you do not have to worry about being too neat with your gluing technique. When using epoxy, make certain to work in a well-ventilated area.

Tile Mastic—Also known as ceramic tile adhesive, tile mastic is available at your local hardware store. It works well on all types of surfaces. It usually comes premixed and is very easy to use. Since it is traditionally used in both kitchens and bathrooms, it has a reasonable tolerance to water exposure.

Tile mastic works well with shells and is one of my favorite adhesives to use. It is thick enough to hold onto small and medium sized shells and can be tinted with adhesive paint.

Tile mastic cleans up easily with soap and water; however, it will not wash out of your clothes.

Thinset—This adhesive is also commonly known as polymer-blended dry-set tile mortar. If you expect your project to be exposed to a lot of water or outdoor use, use thinset. Available in gray or white, it comes in powdered form and must be mixed with water. Because it dries fairly quickly, mix only a little at a time in a disposable cup. Thinset is perfect for outdoor projects such as stepping stones, birdbaths, and water fountains.

Adhesive Accessories—You should have on hand an assortment of diposable brushes, putty knives, or spatulas, and notched adhesive spreaders for applying an even amount of adhesive onto the base.

DESIGNING YOUR PICASIETTE PROJECT

Anytime you begin a project, take into consideration how you intend to use it. Will it be used inside or outside? Do you want it to be formal or whimsical? Will it need to be smooth and functional, or can it be rough and messy? Do you want a symmetrical design that incorporates a few patterns that are repeated throughout the project, or do you want several different patterns to be used at random intervals?

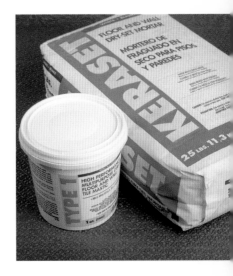

ABOVE: *Shown are tile mastic (also known as ceramic tile adhesive) and thinset (also known as polymer-blended dry-set tile mortar).*

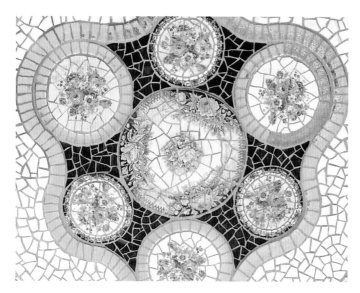

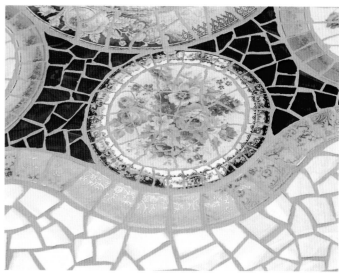

FOREGROUND

If you want a very casual piece, have fun and let the patterns and designs emerge as you go along. Sometimes a loose approach to design can yield unexpected yet satisfying results. However, if you are more comfortable with a controlled design, you may want to do some planning before you begin breaking or adhering the tesserae.

I like to color-coordinate my dishes, so my first step is to gather up a few different patterns that I think would not only look good together but also complement the style and finish of the base. If I am working on a large-scale piece, I also must take into consideration whether or not I have enough of each selected china pattern to complete the design. For instance, when I was planning out the design for the Patio Table on pages 74–75, I wanted to incorporate some Blue Willow into the design. I only had two dessert plates and I needed five or six, so I had to take the Blue Willow out of the equation.

After assessing the materials I had available, I narrowed my options to four china patterns. One plate made up the center circle, which I decided to surround with six other circles. I could have used all of the same dish type (i.e. six dinner plates or six bowls), but I chose to use three dinner plates and three bowls to add interest and movement. I added further interest by keeping the original yellow border for the plates but adding an entirely different border around the bowl centers. I chose this different border because it incorporated both the blue, in keeping with the blue and yellow theme, and the florals. I knew that I would have a lot of yellow edging left over from the bowls, so I decided to enclose the entire center section with a yellow serpentine border. To finish everything off, I used a fourth pattern for the border.

EDGING

There are a number of ways to finish the edges of your mosaic project. There is nothing wrong with using random mosaic pieces and letting the edge of your mosaic turn out however it turns out. However, if you take the time to plan how you want to utilize your china pieces along your edges, you can easily achieve a more finished look.

I usually save the edges of my plates, cups, or bowls to finish the edges of my mosaic. Take advantage of the edge on your china. It usually has a finished, smooth edge that will perfectly finish your piece.

FILLING IN THE FIELD, OR BACKGROUND

Once the foreground and edge patterns are set, you must think about what you want to use to fill in the empty spaces—the field, or background. I usually cover the field with pieces from plain off-white dishes. I find that if I have done a good job of selecting dishes and using them in an interesting pattern, I do not need more activity in the field. However, on the Patio Table, I decided to fill in the central background with blue glass because when I began to place the off-white, it seemed weak next to all that color. Although you have a plan for the design, try to remain open to changing it throughout the process. If you see that your design is not working, simply change it. Just because it looked great in your head or on paper, does not mean it will work when it is actually incorporated into the mosaic.

WORKING PICASIETTE ON A SQUARE OR RECTANGULAR GRID

When designing an intricate pattern, it helps tremendously to draw a grid on the base's surface. You can use the grid as a guideline to determine where you will place the broken plates within the design. Without a grid to work from, it can be very difficult to keep a design in line. I also like to take a plate and draw a circle around it on the surface for placement. Unless otherwise instructed, use the following technique for working picasiette.

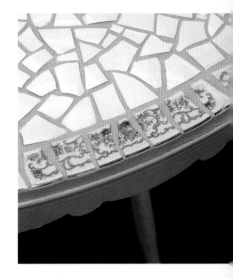

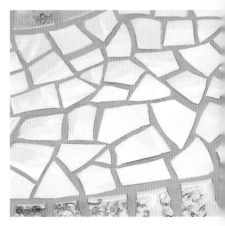

ABOVE TOP: *A single plate border pattern was used for the outside edge on the Patio Table on pages 74–75.*

ABOVE BOTTOM: *The area between the foreground and the edge is called the field. It is usually filled in with off-white china.*

Materials

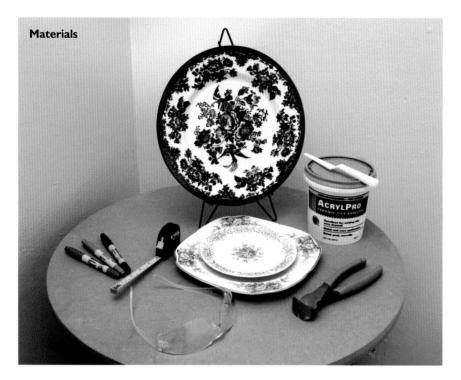

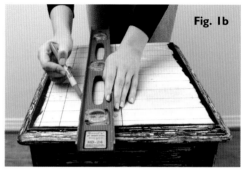
Fig. 1b

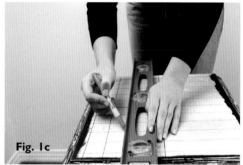
Fig. 1c

Materials needed to apply the design:

- Ceramic tile adhesive
- China: large square plate; small plate
- Permanent marking pens
- Safety glasses
- Spreader for adhesive
- Tape measure
- Tile nippers
- Transferware: large plates (2)

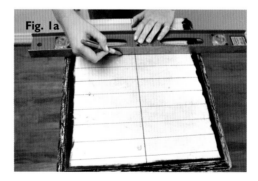
Fig. 1a

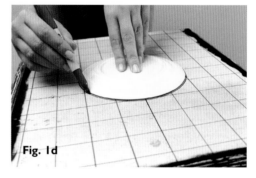
Fig. 1d

INSTRUCTIONS

STEP 1

Mark off the grid. Find and mark the center of the table based on the grid pattern. Use the small plate to draw a circular perimeter for the central plate design. (Figs. 1a–1d)

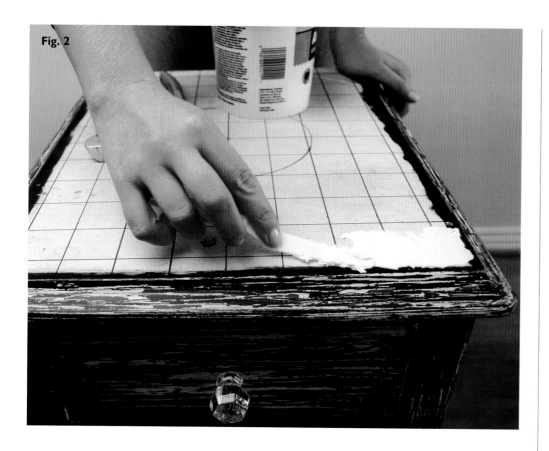

Fig. 2

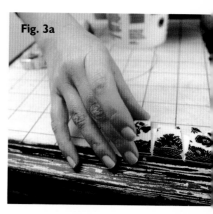

Fig. 3a

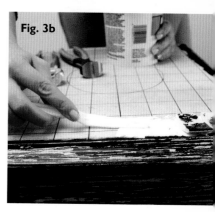

Fig. 3b

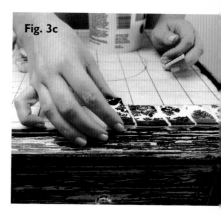

Fig. 3c

STEP 2

Apply mastic in small 3"–4" sections approximately ⅛" thick. Avoid making the band of adhesive wider than the width of the border pieces. If too much mastic is laid down, it will squish up between the applied pieces and fill in the space where the grout must go. (Fig. 2)

STEP 3

Now that you have the first section of adhesive down, you are ready to apply the broken outer border china pieces. Place each piece on top of the mastic as desired. Give it a little twist to ensure that full contact has been made between adhesive and china. Leave a joint that is a minimum of approximately ⅛" between each piece to allow room for grout. A good rule of thumb is a ⅛" minimum and a ¼" maximum space between pieces. (Figs. 3a–3c)

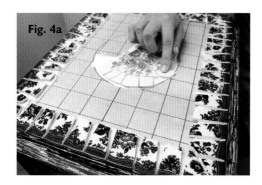
Fig. 4a

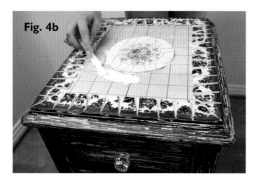
Fig. 4b

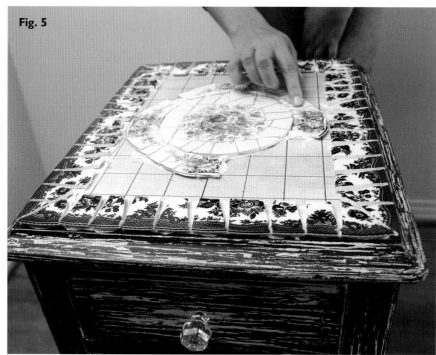
Fig. 5

STEP 4

Adhere the central design. I would suggest that you "dry set" the central design before adhering it with mastic. Dry setting is the process of breaking up a foreground pattern or border edge, then placing it back together in the location that it will be on the finished project to make certain that the spacing is accurate and nothing is out of order. It can be quite frustrating to have half of something glued down and realize that you have misplaced a piece or have messed up the pattern. It is much easier to work out the kinks before adhesive gets involved. (Figs. 4a–4b)

Avoid stopping in the middle of reconstructing a plate center or border as the process often requires a lot of small adjustments to get everything to fit back together just right. Allow enough time to complete the entire piece.

STEP 5

Adhere the inner border around the central design. (Fig. 5)

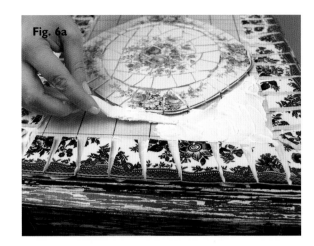

Fig. 6a

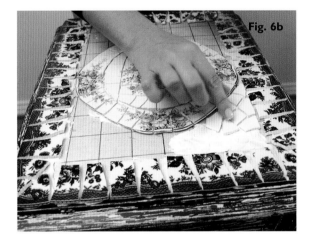

Fig. 6b

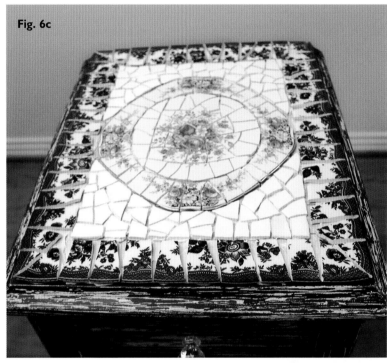

Fig. 6c

STEP 6

Fill in the field with plain off-white china, working one small section at a time to keep the adhesive from drying out. I find that many projects are too time consuming to be completed in one sitting. Restricting the adhesive coverage will create a stopping point if you want to take a break. Remember to leave a joint that is a minimum of approximately ⅛" between each piece of china to allow room for grout. You will likely need to cut the pieces as you fill in the field to be able to fit them into the space between the outer border and the inner border, or central design. (Figs. 6a–6c)

Tip:

Use the grid as a guide for cutting china pieces. The squares can help you to determine whether to cut one or more pieces to fill each grid square. By using the grid in this manner, you will be able to create a uniform design.

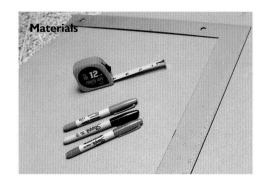

Materials

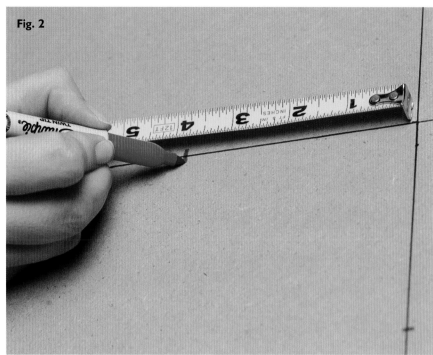

Fig. 2

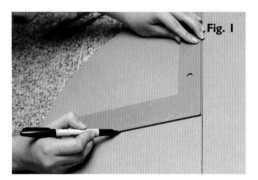

Fig. 1

WORKING PICASIETTE ON A CIRCULAR GRID

Creating a grid layout on a circular surface is a bit complicated; but it is probably even more essential to take the time to measure off a grid on a circular base than on a rectangular or square base. I would never have been able to apply the plates in a symmetrical pattern on the Patio Table on pages 74–75 if I had not first drawn a grid on the tabletop. If you do not take the time to create a radial grid, you are likely to have a lopsided finished product.

INSTRUCTIONS

STEP 1

Draw an axis in the center of the circle. An axis is two lines that are perpendicular to each other and intersect in the center of the circle. This divides the circle into four sections. (Fig. 1)

STEP 2

Mark 4" out from the center point on each line. (Fig. 2)

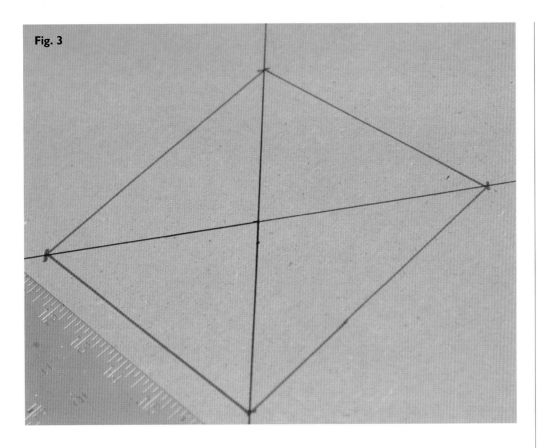

Fig. 3

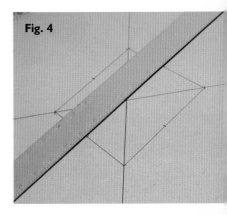

Fig. 4

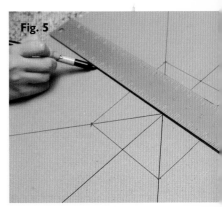

Fig. 5

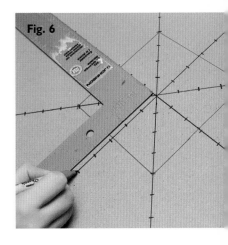

Fig. 6

STEP 3

Connect each point with a straight line to form a square at the center of the circle. (Fig. 3)

STEP 4

Find the center point of each side of the square and place a mark there. (Fig. 4)

STEP 5

Connect the two center points on the opposite sides of the square. This divides the circle into eight sections. (Fig. 5)

STEP 6

Measure and mark every inch from the center of the circle along each radial line. (Fig. 6)

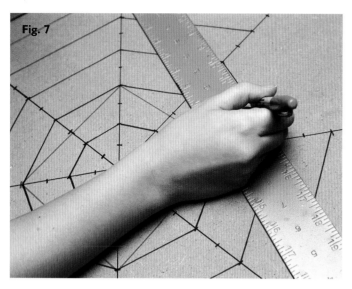

Fig. 7

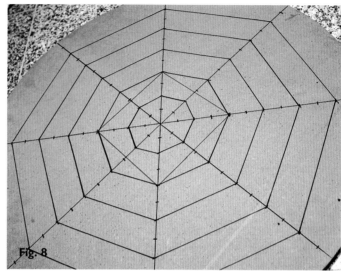

Fig. 8

STEP 7

Draw a connecting line between each radial line at each corresponding set of marks. (Fig. 7)

STEP 8

Now you have created a radial grid on the circular surface that will allow you to lay out the pattern in a symmetrical fashion. These are not to be followed exactly, but use them simply as guidelines to keep the original design on track. (Fig. 8)

GROUTING YOUR PICASIETTE PROJECT

Once you have drawn a grid, completed the design, and applied tesserae onto the surface, you are ready to grout the piece. Unless otherwise instructed, use the following technique for grouting.

The two best pieces of advice I can provide about grouting are: 1) Avoid grouting at night, unless you have excellent lighting, because you will almost always find mistakes in the daylight; and 2) Do not follow the manufacturer's instructions. They work great when working on traditional tile projects but they do not work out so well for picasiette.

Unless otherwise instructed, use sanded grout. Unsanded grout is not the best choice for picasiette because it will easily crack when used to fill in joints ⅛" wide or larger.

Grout is available in a wide array of premixed colors. It is up to you to decide what grout color to use. However, if you want a specific color and you cannot find it premixed, there are a few ways to mix your own colors. You can add colored grout to white grout to get a lighter color than the original. You can mix two different colored grouts together to create a new color. You can also add acrylic paint or powdered tempera to white grout to customize a new color.

Grout is nontoxic, but very caustic; it will dry out your hands and wreak havoc on your manicure. You must wear latex or rubber gloves during the grouting process. Be aware that you can easily go through two or three pairs of gloves during one project.

Mix the grout in a disposable container. It is too difficult and time consuming to clean a grout container. Do not rinse any grout down the drain.

You must allow enough time to complete all of the grouting for the project at one time; do not stop in the middle of the process.

INSTRUCTIONS

STEP 1

Place some of the dry grout into the container and add some water. Stir until smooth like the consistency of peanut butter. The mixture should not drip off of the stir stick when held over the container. Grout most often cracks because the mixture is too wet. If too much water is added, simply allow it to sit for a few minutes until it thickens up, or add a bit more dry grout and stir until smooth. (Figs. 1a–1c)

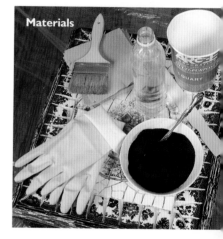

Materials needed for grouting:

- Blue paper shop towels
- Chip paintbrush
- Disposable container
- Grout
- Rubber gloves
- Stir stick
- Water

Materials

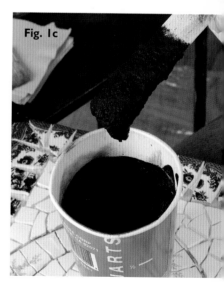

Fig. 1c

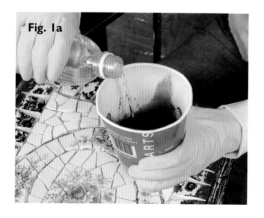

Fig. 1a

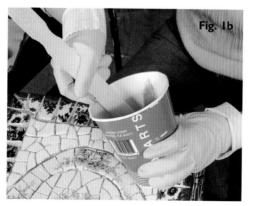

Fig. 1b

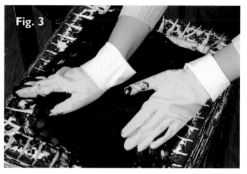

Fig. 2

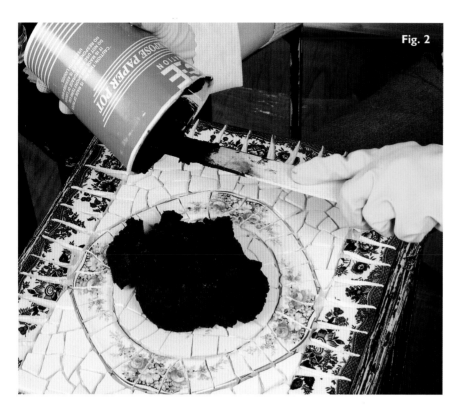

Fig. 3

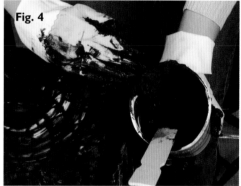

Fig. 4

Tip:

Grout is not only the mortar that fills in the spaces between the tesserae, it is also the element that pulls the mosaic together visually. Experiment with using different grout colors. Notice how white grout mellows the piece; black grout seems to make the colors of the tesserae more vivid; and colored grout gives the mosaic a fun, and playful look.

STEP 2

Pour out a portion of mixed grout onto the surface and spread it around with your gloved hands, making certain to force the grout into all the joints. Sculpt the grout onto the edges to make a nice smooth edge. Generously cover the entire piece. (Fig. 2)

STEP 3

Spread the grout as far as it will go and add more if necessary. You must be thorough and work fast as the cut surfaces of the shards are very absorbent and quickly draw the moisture out of the grout. (Fig. 3)

STEP 4

Once you have covered the entire piece and filled in all of the joints, wipe off as much of the excess grout as possible. Cleaning off grout at this stage will save a lot of work later. Rapidly

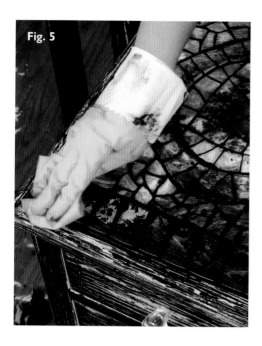

Fig. 5

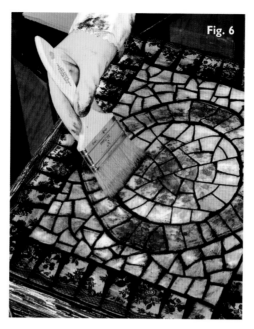

Fig. 6

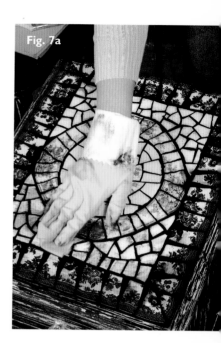

Fig. 7a

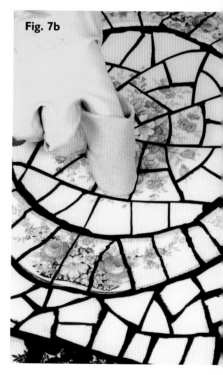

Fig. 7b

rub the entire surface with your gloved hand. Be careful to avoid sharp edges—they will only be smoothed out once the grout has filled in the joints. (Fig. 4)

STEP 5

At this point, change gloves and begin using blue shop towels to rub away excess grout. Blue shop towels are recommended for grout removal because any other type of paper toweling will flake off and stick in the grout. Try to remove as much grout as possible. If you do not get it off now, it will be much more difficult to do so later. (Fig. 5)

STEP 6

Use a large chip paintbrush or small hand broom to whisk away powder throughout this process. (Fig. 6)

STEP 7

Continue rubbing the surface with paper toweling until the grout is as smooth as it can be and the tesserae is as clean as it can be. (Fig. 7a–7b)

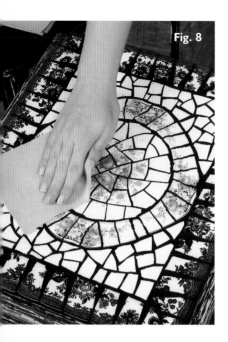
Fig. 8

STEP 8

Allow the piece to rest for 10–15 minutes. Using a soft lint-free cloth, buff away the remaining haze and dust. When you are finished with the grout, throw it and the container away. Do not wash used grout down the drain. (Fig. 8)

STEP 9

Allow the grouted project to set overnight at room temperature. Slow drying will give the piece more strength—do not put it in a warmer place.

STEP 10

The grout can be sealed if you like. Grout sealer is used to keep grout from staining. Sealer is only necessary if you expect the mosaic to come in contact with water, food, or drink. Many quality grouts have an additive that seals the grout and eliminates this extra step. Check the manufacturer's instructions before deciding whether or not to use a sealer.

WORKING WITH MIRRORS

You might wonder why someone would want to go through this lengthy process to age a perfectly good mirror. Simply put, it looks better. A new mirror just does not look right surrounded by vintage china.

A word of caution regarding muratic acid. Be very careful. It is deceptive because it does not burn your skin if you touch it. However, when it comes in contact with moisture, the fumes are horrific—they will burn your eyes and lungs. Wear gloves, goggles, and a mask to avoid breathing in the fumes and contact with your skin and eyes. Remove any jewelry and avoid contact with other metal objects because the chemical will cause them to turn black.

MIRROR ANTIQUING
INSTRUCTIONS
STEP 1

Turn the mirror face down on craft paper or paper toweling and apply paint remover to the mirror back, following the manufacturer's instructions to remove the protective coating. Rinse with clean water, then dry. (Figs. 1a–1e)

Materials needed for mirror antiquing:

- Acrylic paint: black
- Chip paintbrushes: assorted sizes
- Latex gloves
- Mask
- Measuring cups
- Metallic powders: gold, silver
- Mirror
- Muratic acid
- Paint stripper
- Safety glasses
- Scraper
- Sizing
- Sponge
- Water

Materials

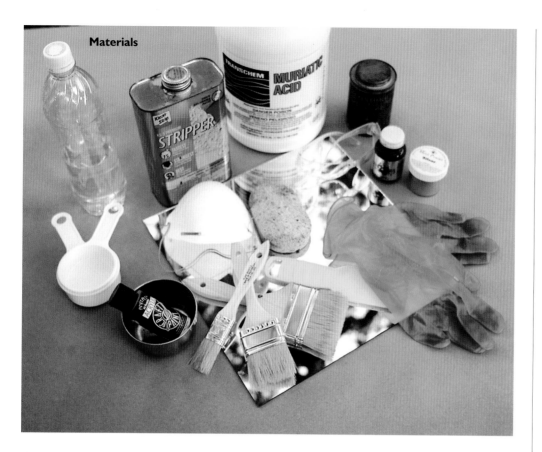

Fig. 1c

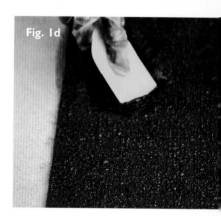

Fig. 1d

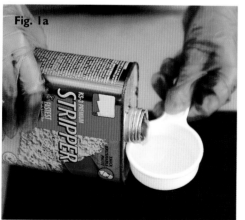

Fig. 1a

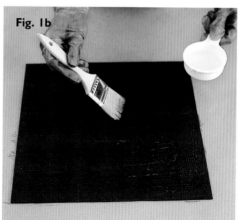

Fig. 1b

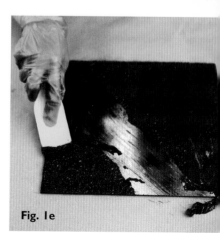

Fig. 1e

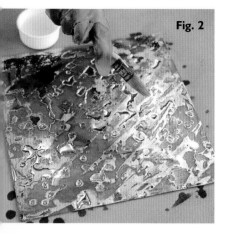

Fig. 2

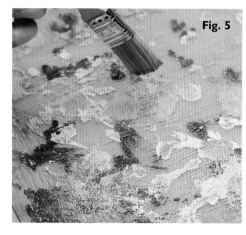

Fig. 5

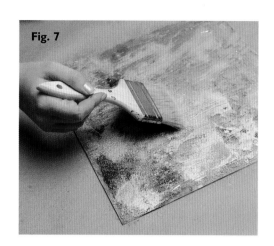

Fig. 7

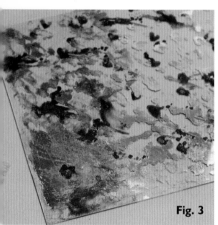

Fig. 3

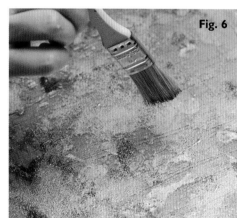

Fig. 6

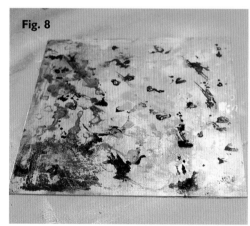

Fig. 8

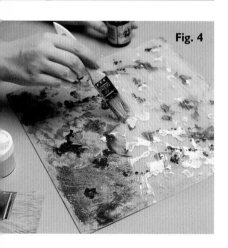

Fig. 4

STEP 2

Use a chip paintbrush to spatter muratic acid over approximately two-thirds of the surface. Once black spots and silvering deterioration begin to appear, you should be able see through the glass to the craft paper underneath. Submerge the entire piece of glass in clean water to neutralize the acid. (Fig. 2)

STEP 3

Dry the back of the mirror, using a soft towel. Mix water with black paint in a 1:1 ratio. Use a wet chip brush to spatter spots randomly over the entire surface. Allow to dry. (Fig. 3)

STEP 4

Apply sizing over the entire surface. Allow to sit for approximately 15 minutes. (Fig. 4)

STEP 5

Wear a mask when working with metal powders. Apply silver powder by dipping a clean, dry brush into the pot and tapping it above the surface. Avoid touching the mirror with the brush because you will get sizing on the brush, which will cause the powder will stick to the brush instead of the mirror. Do not cover the entire surface with silver. (Fig. 5)

STEP 6

Repeat Step 5 with gold powder. Fill in blank areas to cover the entire surface. (Fig. 6)

STEP 7

Using a clean, dry brush, softly brush over the entire surface. This will spread the powder and ensure full adhesion. (Fig. 7)

STEP 8

Now you have transformed a new mirror into one that looks very old and well worn. (Fig. 8) You can see the layers that we created with reverse painting.

Layer 1—What was left of original mirror finish

Layer 2—Age spots created with thinned black paint

Layer 3—Silver powder

Layer 4—Gold powder

The amount of the gold or silver powder used is up to you. If you want a more silvery look, apply more silver. If you want a more gold look, apply more gold. You could also only use one color. If you really want to get wild, go to an art supply store where you can choose from a wide variety of colored metallic powders including reds, blues, and greens.

Another technique that is a bit simpler is to start out with a plain piece of glass, skip Steps 1–3, and start with Step 4. The end result will look more like metallic tile, or smalti, than an aged mirror.

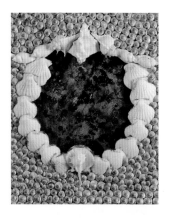

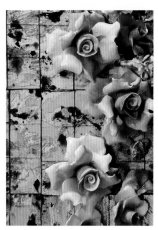

ABOVE TOP: *The Frieze Trumeau Mirror on pages 110–111 uses an antiqued mirror for its centerpiece. Shells are then adhered around it to resemble an architectural pattern.*

ABOVE BOTTOM: *The Victorian Door on pages 88–89 is made up of 1"-square pieces of antiqued mirror and accented by delicate porcelain roses.*

Materials

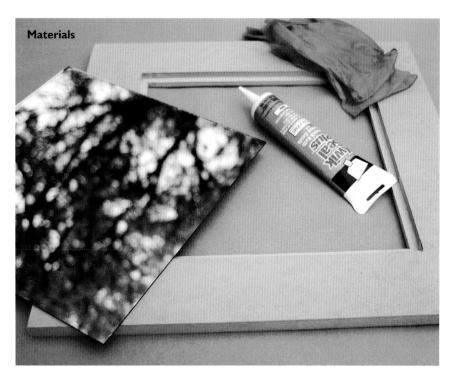

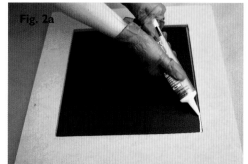

Fig. 2a

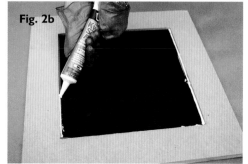

Fig. 2b

Materials needed for mirror installation:

- Clear silicone adhesive
- Frame
- Latex gloves
- Mirror

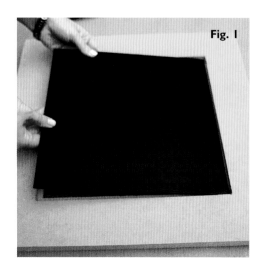

Fig. 1

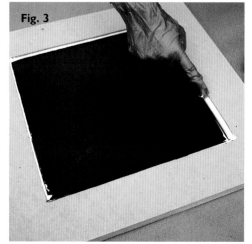

Fig. 3

MIRROR INSTALLATION

There are several pieces in this book that require knowledge of how to install a mirror within a frame. Some of them use an antiqued mirror and some simply replace an old mirror or glass panel with a new mirror.

INSTRUCTIONS

STEP 1

Place the frame face down on a flat surface. Insert the mirror, face down. (Fig. 1)

STEP 2

Apply clear silicone in the space between the mirror edge and frame. (Figs. 2a–2b)

STEP 3

With a gloved finger, press the silicone into the crevice and remove any excess with paper toweling. (Fig. 3)

STEP 4

Silicone will be white when wet, but as it dries it will become clear. Allow to sit undisturbed for 12–24 hours.

STEP 5

Once the silicone is dry, your mirror should be very secure. However, you may still want to apply a paper backing or thin piece of wood to protect the back of the mirror from being scratched.

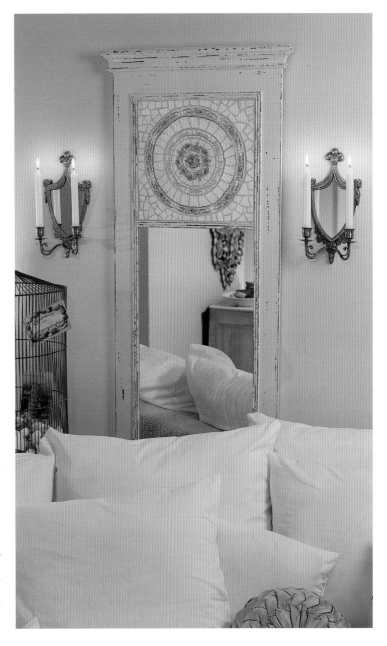

ABOVE: *The China Trumeau Mirror on pages 94–95 shows one pairing of a mosaic with a mirror.*

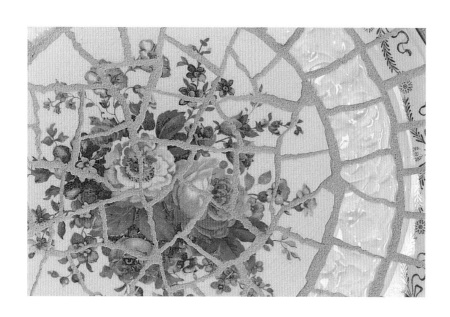

Silver Platter

OPPOSITE: *This silver platter required breaking one floral-patterned dinner plate for the central design. Because the platter is much larger in diameter than the plate, it makes a perfect frame for the planned mosaic.*

How can you transform a battered silver tray with picasiette?

A mosaic is a fabulous way to dress up a worn silver tray. Simply cover the inner area of the tray with beautiful china and you have a new, pretty serving tray. Although this is a small-scale project, it requires breaking four different plates to achieve the different patterns and textures in the design—you must be willing to sacrifice the china pieces you have stashed away for the success of the design. Take your time working out the design and make certain to use an adhesive that sticks to metal.

Additional project ideas include covering a wooden charger or bed tray; an entire tea service—teapot, creamer, and sugar bowl—could also serve as bases for creating mosaics.

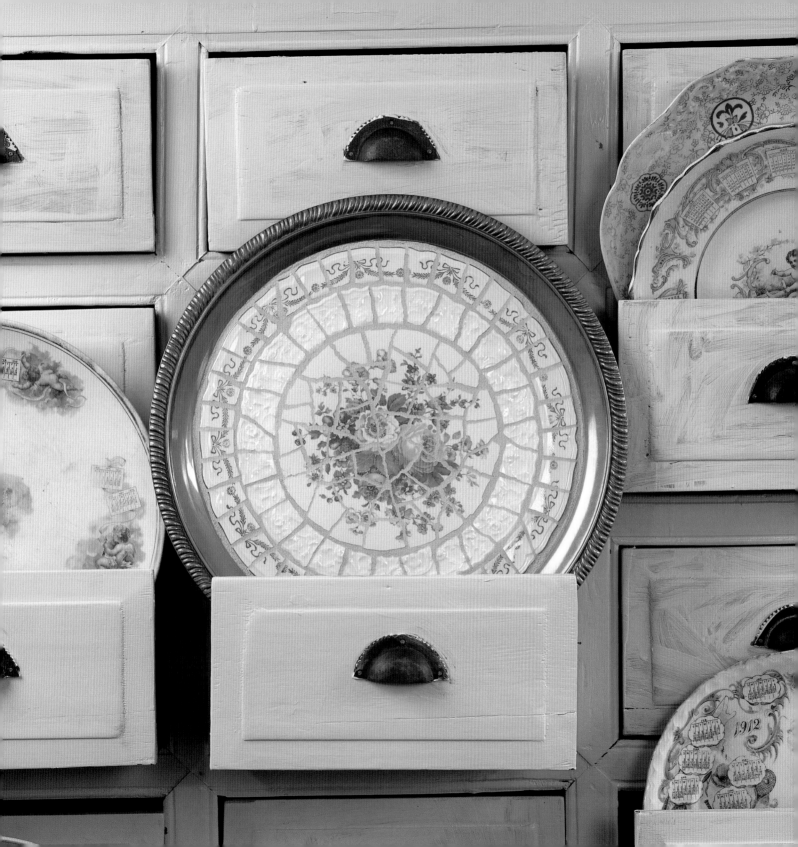

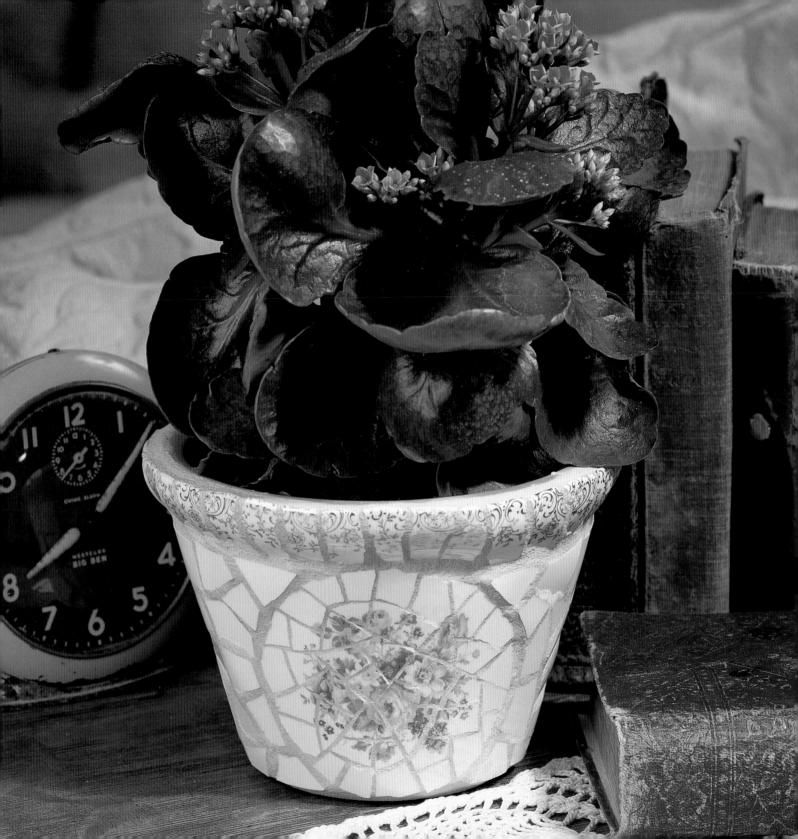

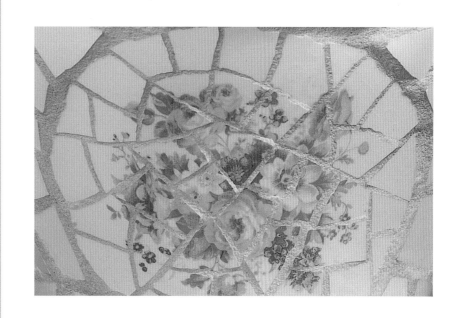

Flowerpot

How can you cover a curved vertical surface?

When working with a flowerpot or similarly shaped item, it is recommended that you first apply a plate border to the rim of the pot and allow it to dry. You may find that turning the pot upside down will keep the tesserae from sliding off as it is drying. Once the top edge is dry the entire piece with be easier to work with. When working small pots, it may be easier to hold the project in one hand while the other applies the tesserae. However, for larger pots, you will have to rest the pot on its side. To keep it from rolling around, wedge a large shard on each side. Be certain to allow tesserae to dry before working on another section.

OPPOSITE: *The sides of an ordinary terra-cotta pot are covered with a floral-patterned dessert plate. The rim of the pot is covered with the gilded edge of a dinner plate.*

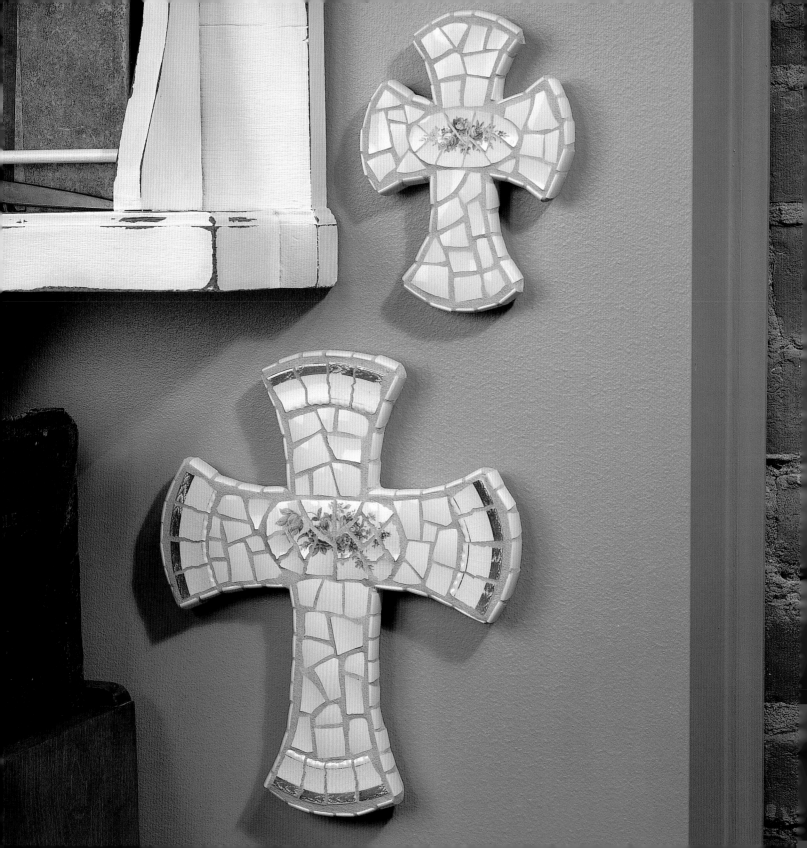

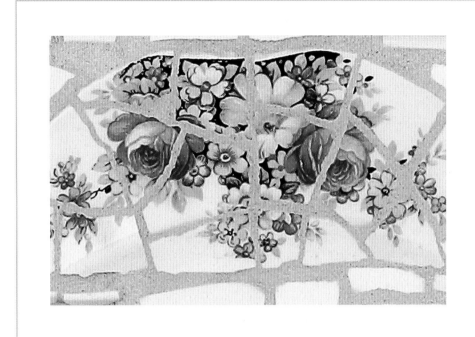

Cross

How can you create a shape that you can't find ready-made?

Sketch out the shape and enlarge or reduce it to the size you wish. I decided to design a cross shape that would lend itself to being covered with chipped china. Transfer the Cross Pattern on page 48 or design of your choice to ¾"-thick MDF and cut out with a scroll saw or jigsaw. You could use random pieces in a scattered informal pattern or follow my lead to create a more structured look. I designed the shape and size of the cross to accommodate two easily attainable china elements. The first is the floral motif that is often found either on the inside or outside of a teacup—use this for the center of the cross. The second is the border from a dessert plate—cover the curve of the outside edge of the cross shape with these smooth pieces. Fill in the legs of the cross with off-white china.

OPPOSITE: A finished edge was incorporated into this design. Precut and save edge pieces of the same pattern in dedicated containers so they are readily available when you would like to work a piece that requires a finished edge.

CROSS PATTERN

ACTUAL SIZE FOR SMALL
ENLARGE 175% FOR LARGE

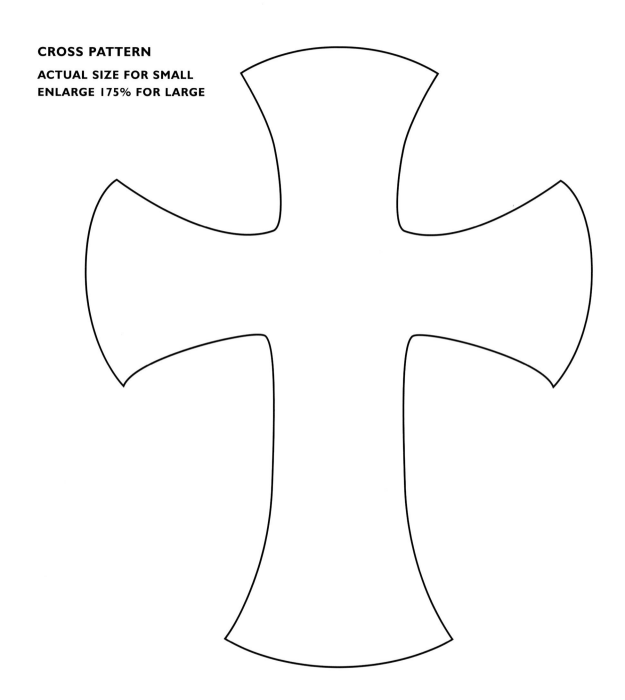

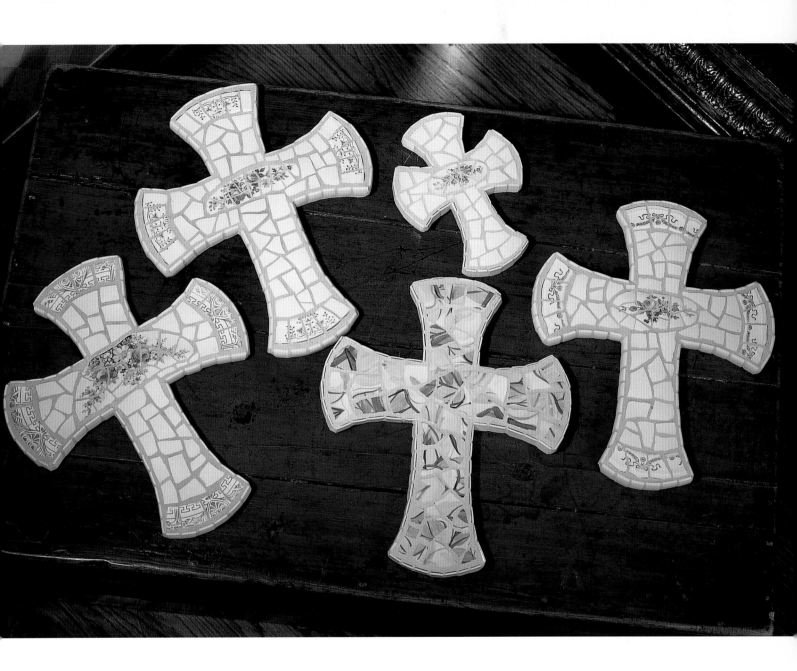

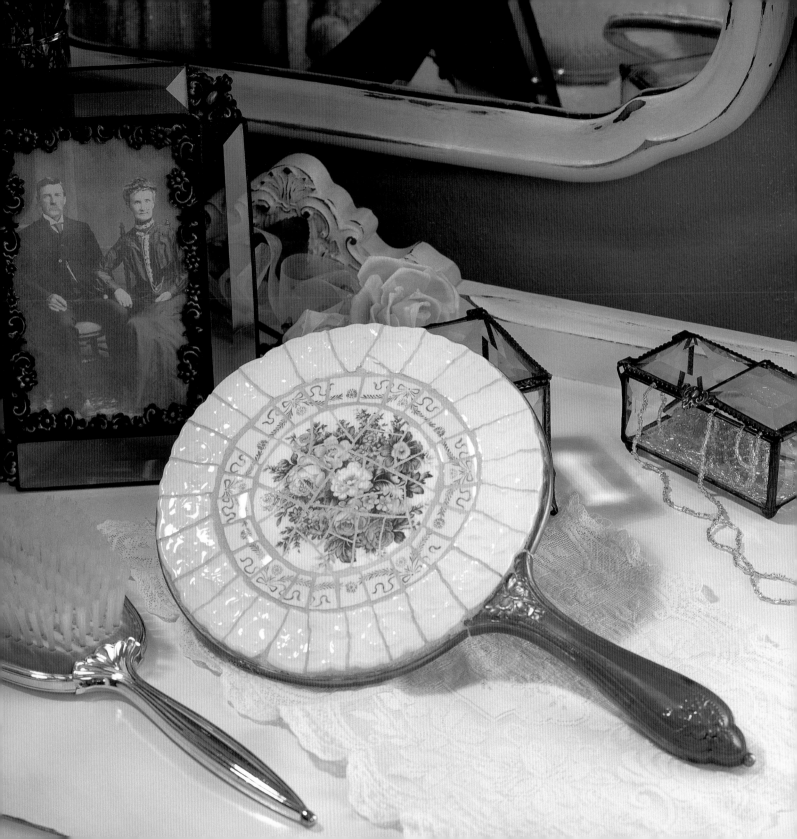

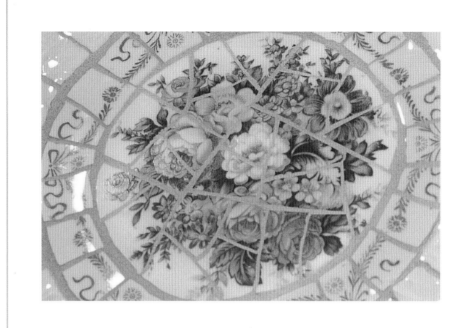

Hand Mirror

Should you pass up garage-sale "fixer-uppers?"

No. In fact, you should look for objects that are in need of a facelift. These include items such as hand mirrors, jewelry boxes, canister lids, picture frames, etc. Old hand mirrors like this can be found at yard sales and thrift shops, and they are very simple to work with. Select a china pattern that has a scale and size appropriate for the shape of the mirror back. For this piece, a dessert-plate center fits perfectly and is surrounded by two additional plate borders. Begin the design at the center and work outward. Use tile mastic to adhere the china pieces onto the metal surface and grout as usual.

OPPOSITE: *If the metal base you are applying a mosaic to has a smooth untextured finish, you must first prepare the surface so your tesserae will adhere properly. You can give the surface "tooth" by scratching the surface with rough-grit sandpaper.*

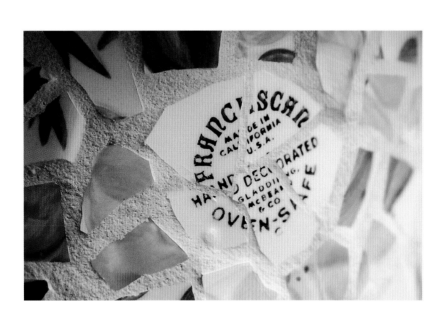

Virginia's Birdhouse

ABOVE: *The maker's mark is included on the back of the body of the birdhouse. With this pattern, you must be careful to select a piece from an older generation; remember to look at the mark and avoid those that are microwave safe because they do not break as well.*

Should you break collectible plates?

Of course you should use your best judgement when breaking any dish, but as far as I am concerned, nothing is sacred. This charming birdhouse was made for a collector of Franciscan Desert Rose who also has a passion for collecting birdhouses. A popular collectible, Franciscan Desert Rose first bloomed in 1941, and its appeal has thrived ever since. When selecting from a collectible china pattern, be mindful of the differences between pieces from the 1940s and pieces that are being manufactured today. Not only are they more sculpted than earlier ones, they are also formulated for modern-day use and are subsequently harder to break.

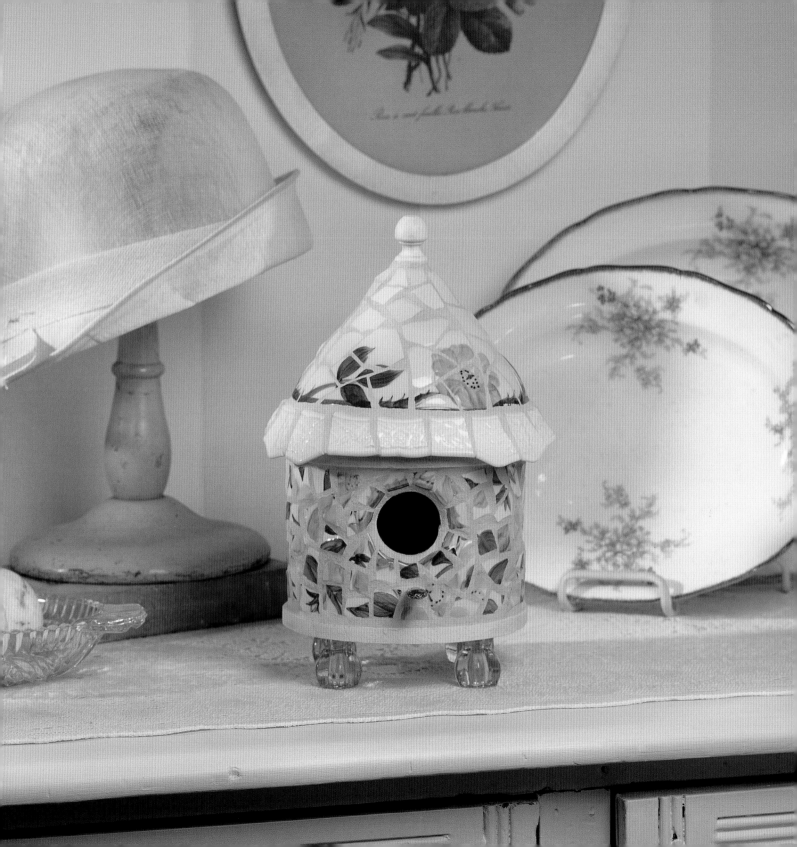

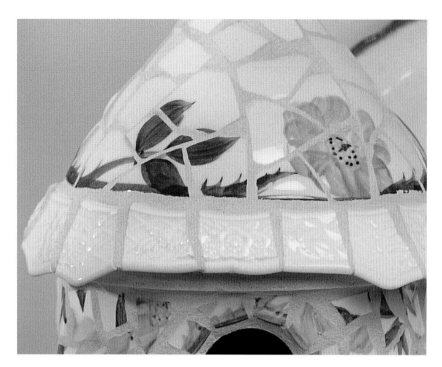
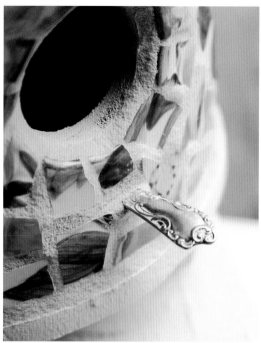

TECHNICAL DISCUSSION

The base for this birdhouse is a typical wooden frame found at a local craft store. I selected this circular design because of its graceful charm, but I still felt it needed a few extra embellishments. First, I removed the plain wooden perch that it came with and drilled a hole so that I could attach a spoon handle later. Then I adhered a small wooden finial onto the top of the roof with construction adhesive. This type of finial is easy to find in the wood section of your local craft store.

Next, I applied the mosaic to the roof and body of the birdhouse, making certain to use smooth-edged pieces along the inside edge of the door.

I used the edge of a square-shaped plate to create the border for this birdhouse roof. By using a square plate rather than a round one, I was able to create a little extra interest along the roof line. I found a tiny salt spoon to replace the wooden perch, which I installed with construction adhesive. After everything had dried, I grouted the birdhouse and attached vintage-style glass drawer pulls for feet.

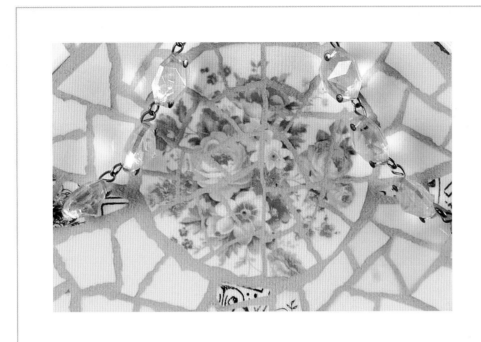

Picture Frame

How can you create your own antique-looking picture frame?

First, determine how large you would like it to be by measuring the size of the art you wish to frame. Enlarge the Picture Frame Pattern on page 57 so the inner opening fits this measurement. Transfer the design onto ¾"-thick MDF and cut it out with a scroll saw or jigsaw. Cover the wood with your choice of china.

The sample shown is 9½" x 13½" and uses a floral pattern for its central motif, accentuated by gilded pieces in selected areas. Somehow, it seemed inappropriate to put a shiny new photograph in this frame so I chose to display it on a large antique mirror, embellished with a chain of crystals and framing an antique broach.

ABOVE & PAGE 56: *A mosaic need not be expensive to look rich. Keep in mind that you can usually find chipped or cracked plates at discounted prices in patterns that might otherwise be beyond your budget. This is especially true of much-sought-after antique pieces.*

PICTURE FRAME PATTERN

ENLARGE 225%

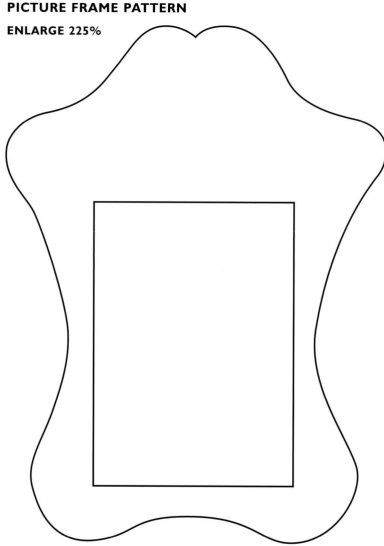

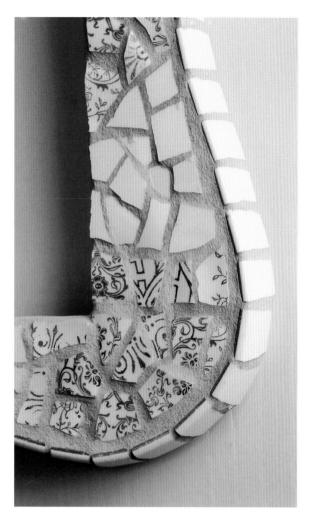

ABOVE LEFT: *Special care is taken to select, cut, and place pieces from the edge of a plate along the side edge of the frame.*

TECHNICAL DISCUSSION

The surface of this picture frame is covered with raw-edged china pieces all the way to the edge of the frame. I applied small pieces from a plate edge vertically along the side of the frame with the smooth edge flush with the front of the mosaic. This creates a smooth outside edge.

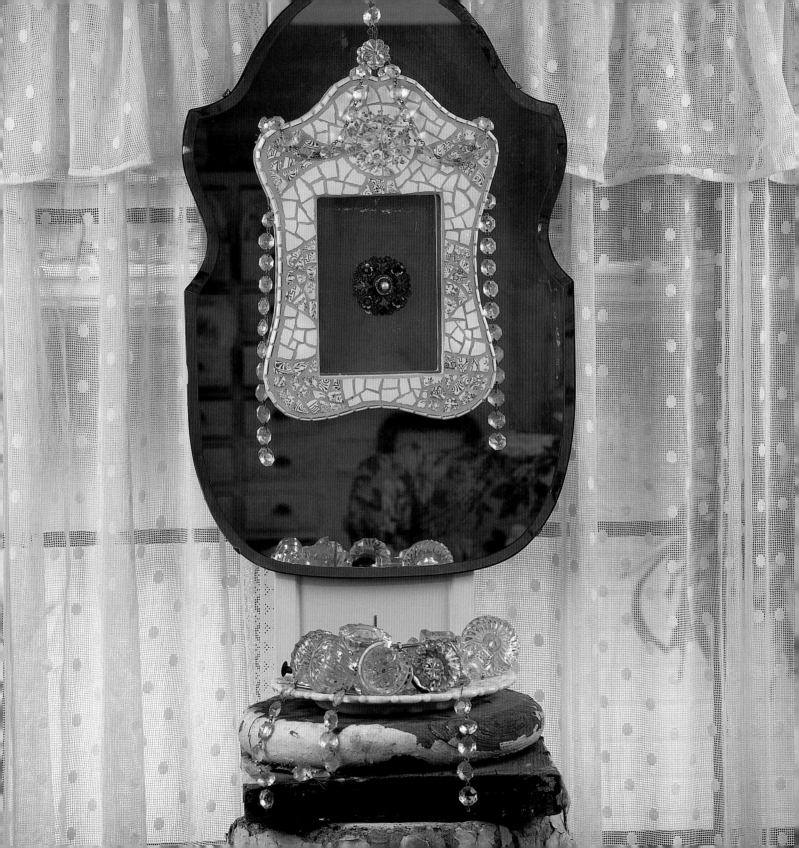

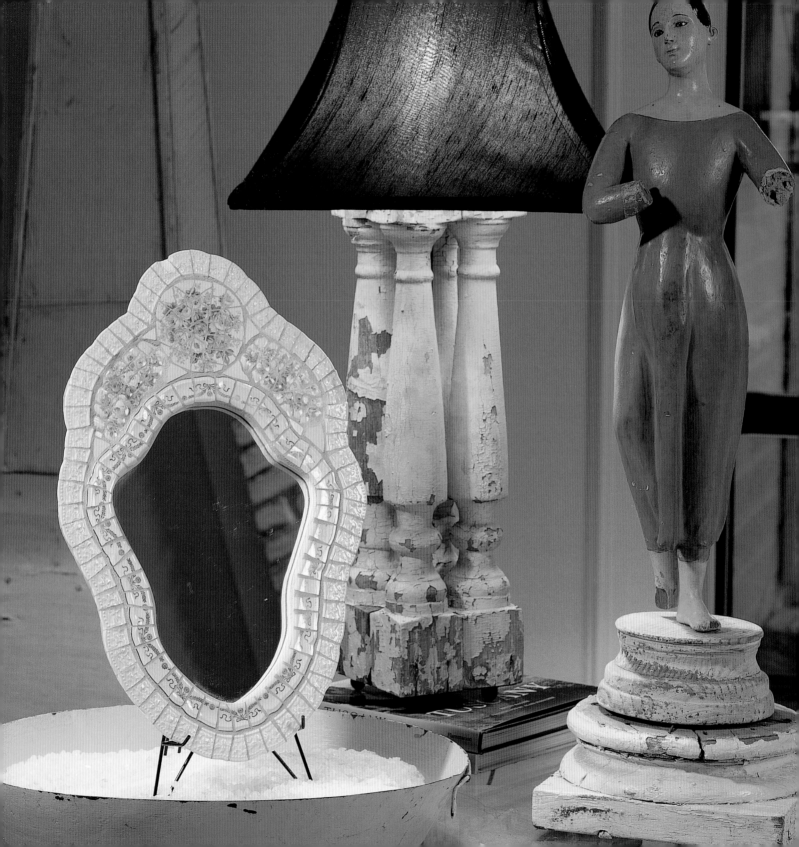

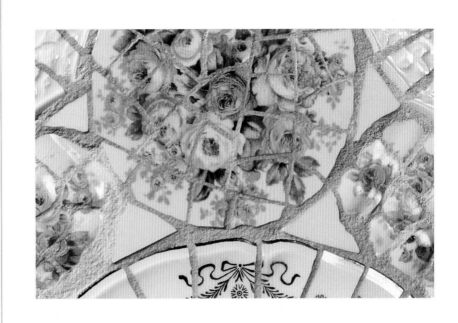

Boudoir Mirror

How can you design a frame for an oval accent mirror?

Precious accent mirrors like this are perfect for picasiette application. Enlarge the Boudoir Mirror Pattern on page 60 to the desired size and have a mirror cut to fit the frame. Transfer the design onto ¾"-thick MDF and cut it out with a scroll saw or jigsaw. Cover the wood with your choice of china, giving special attention to the curves of the inside border so they not only frame the face of the viewer but also allow the plate borders to maintain their natural curve.

The sample shown is 11" x 17½". A larger version of this pattern would make an enchanting mirror for a powder room.

OPPOSITE: *The design for this mirror frame requires one floral-patterned dessert plate for the central motif and oblong floral patterns from two matching teacups for placement on each side. It also uses two plate borders for the inside and outside edges. Like most mosaics, the design is worked from the center outward, placing the inside border first, then the floral motifs, and finally the outside border.*

BOUDOIR MIRROR PATTERN

ENLARGE 250%

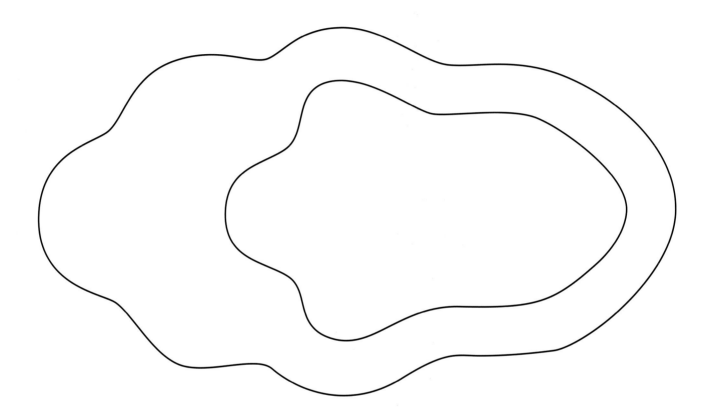

ABOVE: *Cut edge pieces from bowl borders to take advantage of their vertical curved shape. Adhere border pieces with the smooth side facing downward. Then you can use a different plate border for the top edge. I prefer to let the outside edge of the plate border hang over about ⅛" beyond the frame edge.*

TECHNICAL DISCUSSION

This mirror frame was designed to accommodate the center of a dessert plate, two cups, and two plate borders. You can often find cups that have an oblong floral motif either on the inside or outside. I recommend that you first apply the inside border. This will determine where you place the bottom edge of the central circular design. Apply the central circular design, then the two cup motifs on either side. Next apply the outside border. Fill in the field with plain off-white china. Grout as usual.

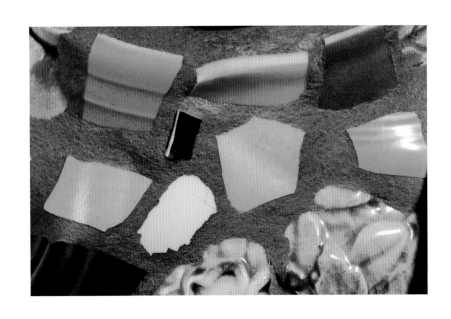

Olive Oil Jug

Can you use art pottery in a mosaic?

ABOVE & PAGE 62: *Because a typical piece of California art pottery is made up of rounded surfaces, the rounded broken pieces that result are best suited for curved bases such as this olive oil jug.*

When a fellow antique dealer handed me a large cardboard box full of broken California art pottery, I knew I could put the pieces to good use on a project such as this. Pottery is more difficult to break than china, but if you are not too particular about the sizes and shapes you end up with, it can be a wonderful source of tesserae. This olive oil jug is a good example of a shard-art piece that has smooth edges. The top edge is finished off nicely with a selection of finished ceramic edges from the original piece of pottery. Notice also that only the upper section of the olive oil jug is covered with pottery pieces and the grout is almost seamlessly blended onto the surface.

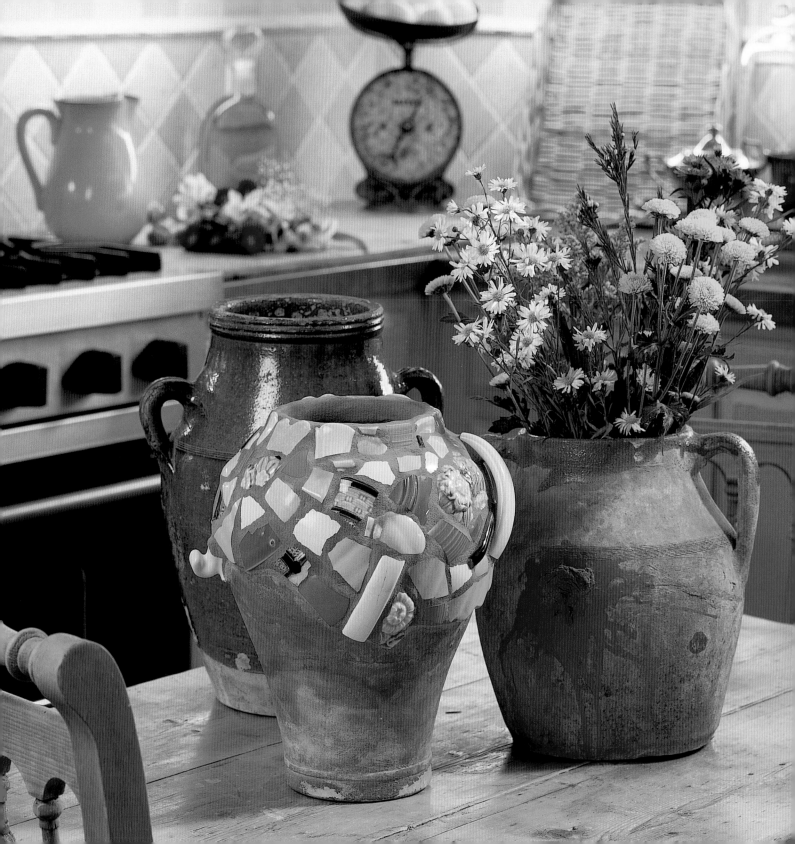

RIGHT: *Different shapes and colors of pottery are given some uniformity by adhering them onto the olive oil jug with approximately the same amount of space between them.*

FAR RIGHT TOP: *For visual effect, smaller pieces are placed near the top edge and grow larger as they work down the jug.*

FAR RIGHT MIDDLE: *A yellow ceramic teapot handle is included in the mosaic while majolica-style pottery motifs are used to provide a small focal point.*

FAR RIGHT BOTTOM: *A ceramic leaf is reconstructed to provide yet another point of interest.*

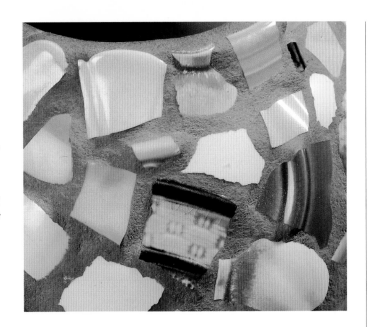

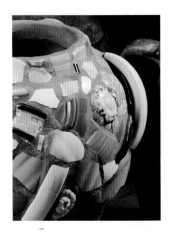

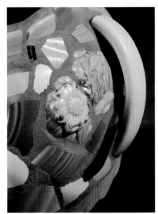

TECHNICAL DISCUSSION

Several different pieces of California art pottery were used to create this shard-art piece. I selected several unrelated pieces that complemented each other and the color of the base. Although I was attempting to create the look of an uncontrolled, spontaneous work of shard art, I still took some time to plan specific elements. I made certain that all of the pieces along the opening of the vase had a smooth finished edge. I also wanted to have a few interesting groupings distributed throughout the mosaic. The yellow arched piece is the handle from a teapot. Tucked just under that is a cluster of majolica-style pottery. Across from the cluster is a pottery leaf. Instead of breaking all of these pieces into smaller bits and spreading them throughout the piece, I treated each one as a small focal point. Planning can make all the difference—even in an asymmetrical shard-art project.

Although I did not expect this piece to be exposed to a lot of water, I used thinset to adhere the shards. The surface of the olive oil jug was very powdery and I found that the thinset grabbed onto it better than mastic would. To finish everything off, I selected a grout color that complemented the entire piece—a good example of using grout color to unify the base and the mosaic.

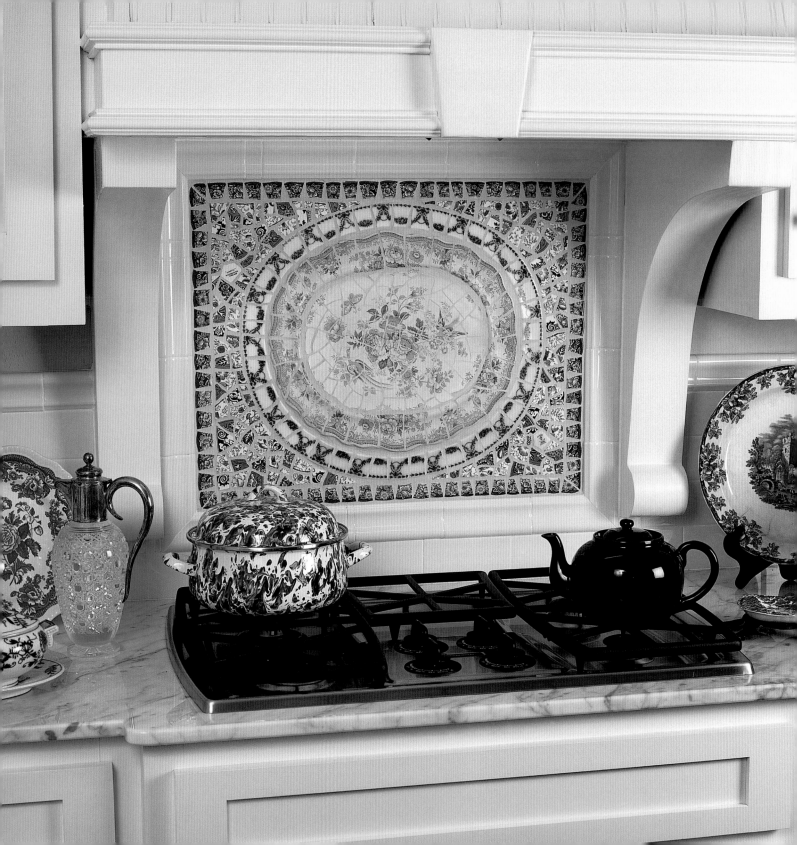

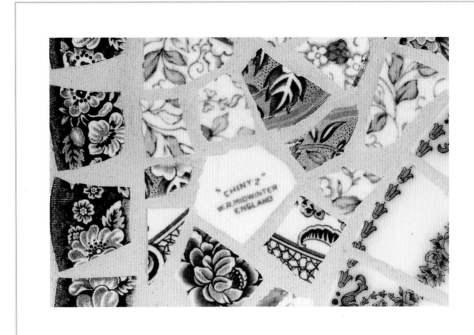

Blue Transferware Backsplash

How can you put a china serving platter to good use?

Any vertical surface is well-suited for the application of a broken serving platter because it is not required to be smooth. A friend of mine, who asked me to create this backsplash over her stove, had friends that were on a buying trip in England. Fortunately for us, they found this gorgeous Asiatic Pheasant platter in the perfect shade of blue. Unfortunately for them, they broke it before making their way home; but we were glad to take it off their hands. Pieces of chintz and blue transferware are used to complement the central platter design and fill in the field of the backsplash design. Two additional pieces of blue transferware provide an inside and outside border.

OPPOSITE & ABOVE: *Sometimes a design will allow the use of patterned china for filling in the field, or empty space between the central design and the edge. Two different patterns, randomly broken and placed were used for this project. Notice the inclusion of the maker's mark.*

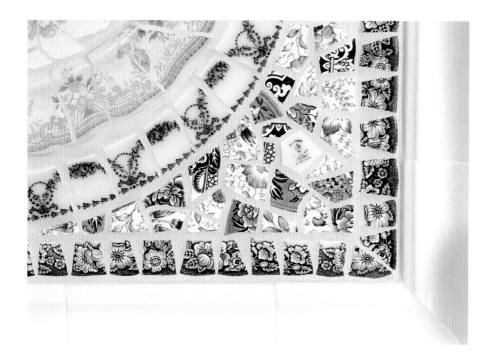

ABOVE: *This design is monochro-matic. The placement of colors in this piece goes from light to dark, from the center to the outside edge.*

TECHNICAL DISCUSSION

This backsplash is an example of a mosaic that incorporates traditional tile and picasi-ette. The entire design was built around the reconstruction of a broken platter. It was framed by a tile molding.

First, I found the center of the backsplash and adhered the platter onto the wall with mastic. I then applied the garland border pieces around the platter. After that, I applied the blue transferware pieces along the outer edge of the design for an outside border. Next, I broke up two more pieces of transferware and chintz into small pieces. I filled in all of the empty spaces with these pieces, making certain that they were spread randomly throughout. I also incorporated two maker's marks in the field as a special treat for anyone who pays close attention.

I decided to frame the entire design with a tile molding. Using commercial moldings is an easy way to finish a mosaic. You could also use this technique on a mosaic that is on a tabletop.

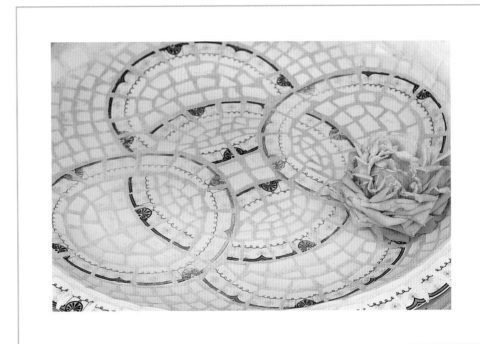

Encrusted Birdbath

Where can you find inspiration for a mosaic?

P ay attention to your surroundings. Take note of the patterns in nature and in architecture. I designed this birdbath after returning from a vacation to Paris where I was enchanted by the intertwining circular patterns I saw in a stained-glass window at Notre Dame Cathedral. This piece, made strictly from plate borders and filled in with off-white china, pales by comparison; but I love it because it reminds me of the beauty I saw in Paris. You may have a particular element in the architecture of your home or perhaps in the design of the iron or brickwork of your patio that you would like to imitate. You need not reinvent the wheel—simply re-create the design in your mosaic.

ABOVE & PAGE 68: *This pattern of intertwining circles is easy to do in mosaic since you are working with cut pieces that you are able to place as you like. The rings are made from the borders of five plates and the field is filled in with off-white china. Notice how the plate border is also positioned around the entire edge of the birdbath bowl.*

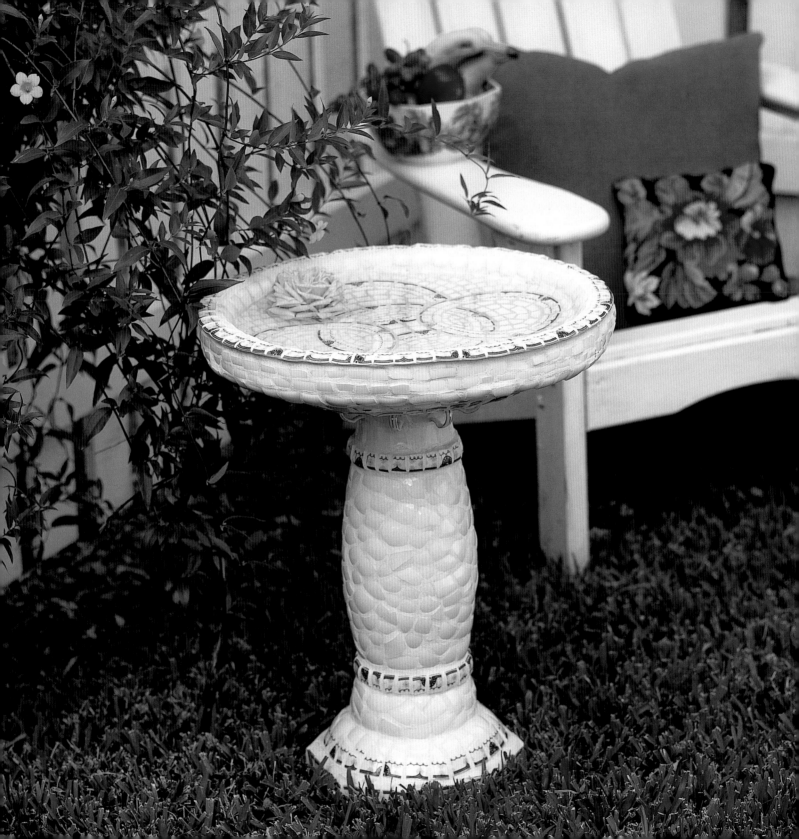

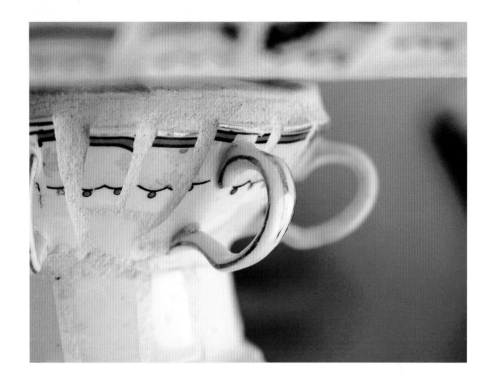

TECHNICAL DISCUSSION

I used a typical concrete birdbath for the base of this project. It had some carving along the outside of the bowl and at the bottom of the base that got in the way of applying a mosaic. This problem was solved by mixing up some thinset and using a gloved hand to smear it into the carving. Just enough was applied to create a smooth surface and allowed to dry thoroughly. If you remember this technique, you will be able to find a use for almost any concrete piece you come across—even if it has an intricately carved design.

Since this piece is going to spend most of its life outside and filled with water, I used thinset to adhere the broken china pieces.

I used cups instead of plates to cover the pedestal base because it had graceful curves that I did not want to lose by covering it with flat plates. By the time I finished breaking up enough cups to cover the entire pedestal, I had 15–20 cup handles left over. I decided to place a ring of them around the top of the pedestal just to add a little whimsy.

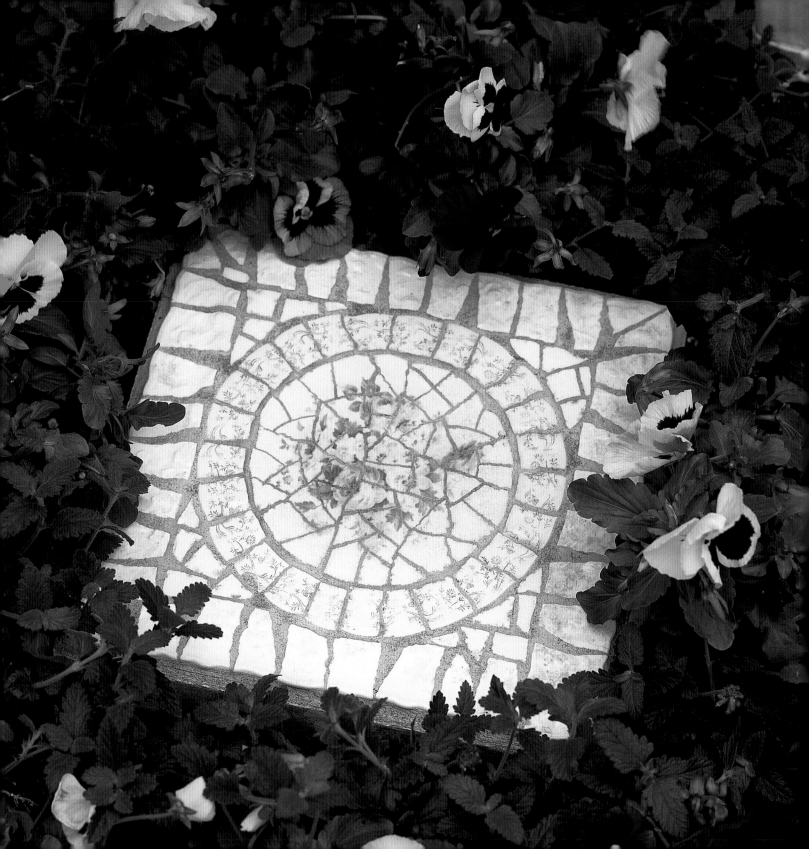

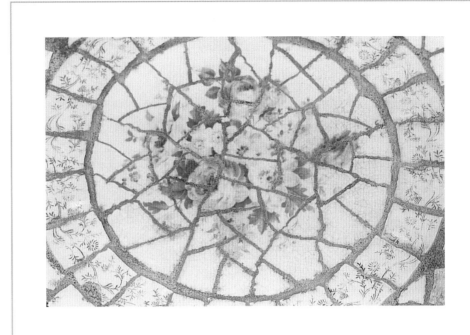

Stepping Stone

How can you use a round pattern on a square surface?

Simply center a round pattern (in this case, an entire plate) on a square surface, frame up the outside edge, and fill in the empty corner spaces—a perfect example of a "round peg in a square hole." Even if you have chosen to create an intricate design, a stepping stone can be started and finished in one morning and find itself basking in the garden sun by mid-afternoon. Because this piece is used outdoors, you must make certain to use thinset as your adhesive.

Where you place your stepping stone may influence how much attention you give to the side edges. If it will rest on the ground with the edges showing, cover them, too.

OPPOSITE: *Although the completed stepping stone can be left outdoors in spring, summer, and fall, you will want to bring it indoors during the winter because mosaics are not completely resistant to water. If any water works its way under the tesserae and freezes, the expansion could cause the tesserae to pop off the piece.*

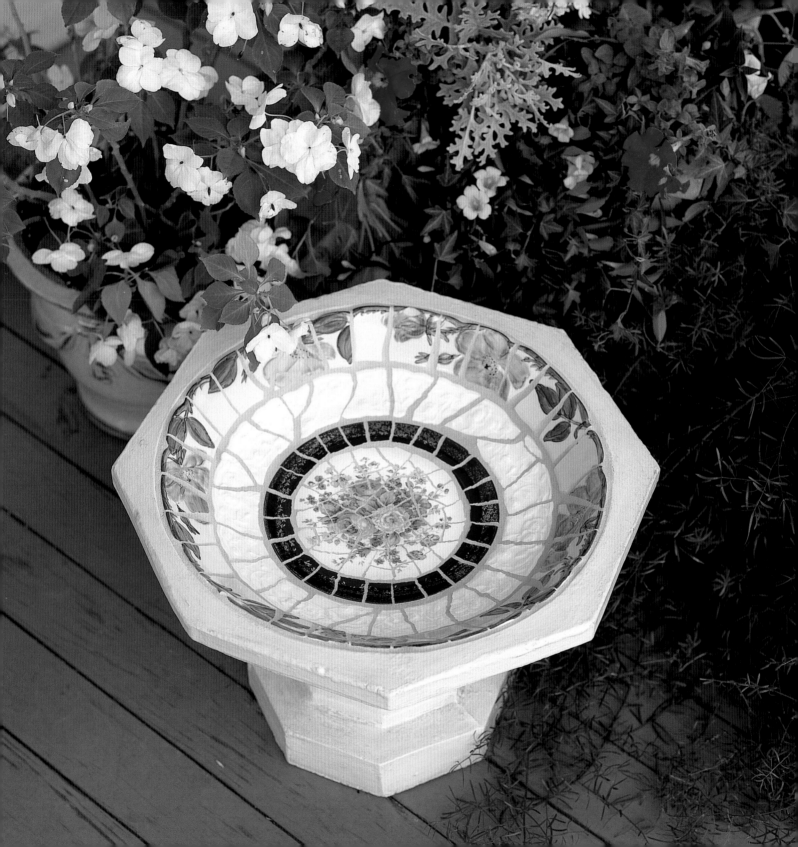

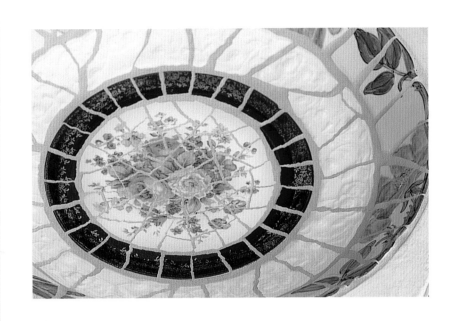

English-style Birdbath

How can you cover a concave surface?

t helps to select an adhesive that will set up quickly so the china pieces do not slip out of place. Start with thinset as your adhesive since it is recommended for outdoor use. On this piece, only the inside of the birdbath bowl is covered. When you are applying the tesserae to the sidewalls of the birdbath, it is especially important that your thinset not be too runny. If it is not thick enough to hold the china pieces in place, do not add more thinset to the mix. Make a new batch instead. Allow the adhesive to dry and grout as usual. It is a good idea to seal the grout after it is dried and buffed because the piece will likely come in contact with water.

OPPOSITE: *This particular piece incorporates both bold and pastel colors—just as you might find in a rambling English country garden. The design shown begins in the center with a floral-patterned dinner plate, surrounded by a burgundy plate border, and a ring of off-white china. It is finished off with pieces cut from bowl edges in the popular Franciscan Desert Rose pattern.*

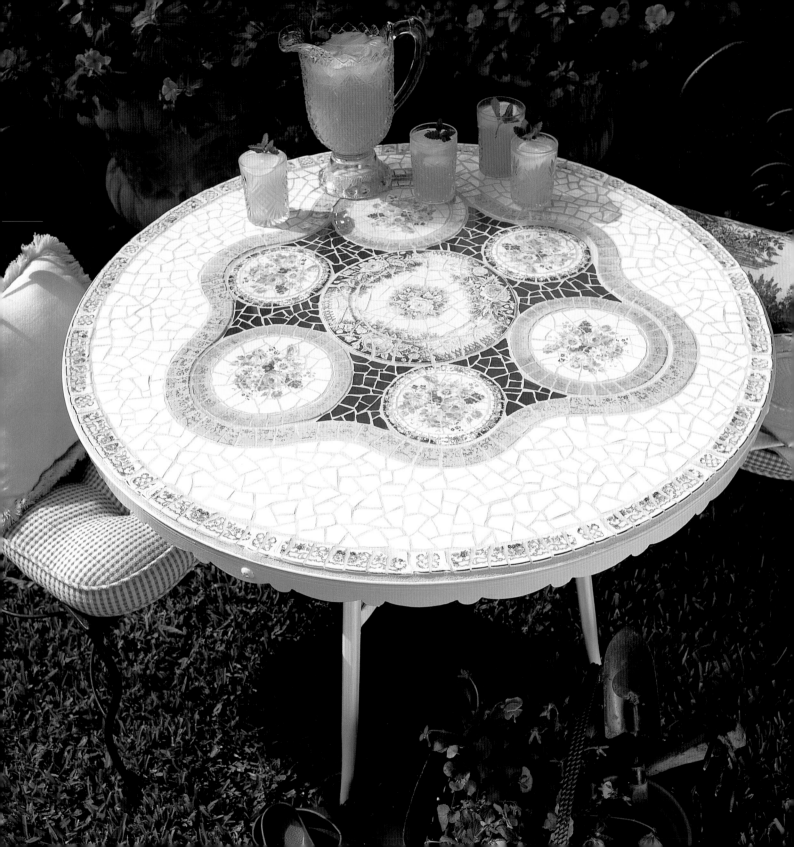

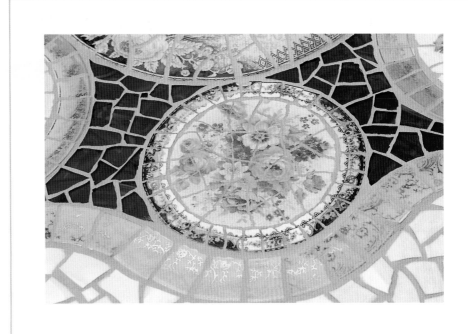

Patio Table

Is there such a thing as too many colors in a design?

I f you are uncertain, consult a color wheel to find two colors that you would like to use as the dominant colors. This should provide you with a starting point. Do not be afraid to "push the envelope" where color is concerned—especially when working on outdoor pieces. For this tabletop, I selected vibrant yellow and cobalt blue pieces. I combined these colors with a floral pattern that contained these two main colors plus a few accent colors. Once positioned on the table, this grouping created an island of explosive color. I surrounded the island by a field of off-white china and enclosed the entire design with another colorful plate border.

OPPOSITE: *To even up a surface that is supposed to be flat, use a flat wood block to press the tesserae into the adhesive once you have completed a section of the design. Apply the pieces for the next section and repeat with the wood block.*

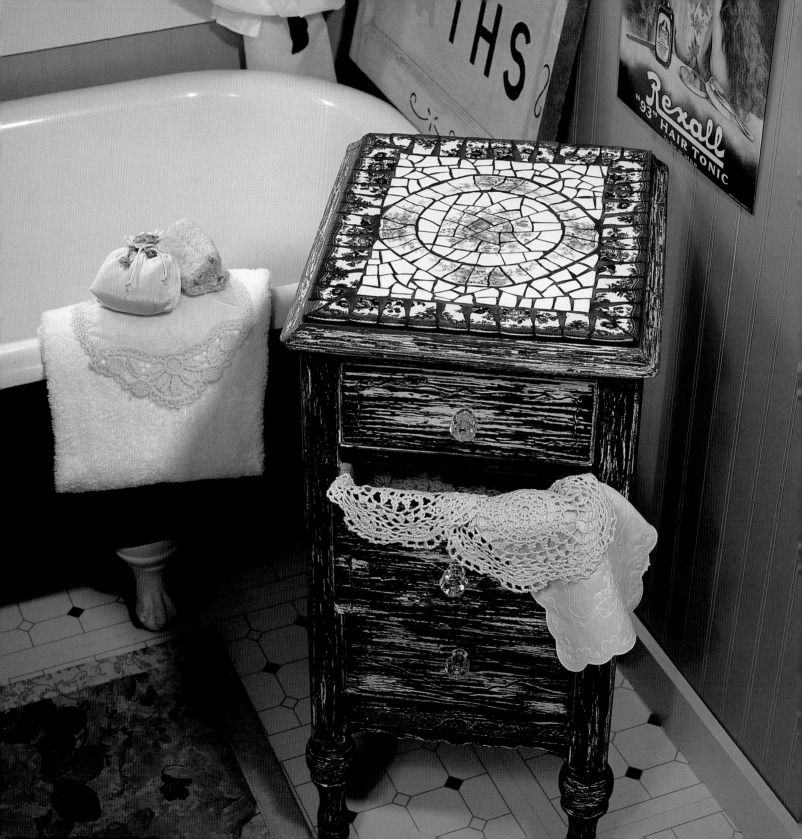

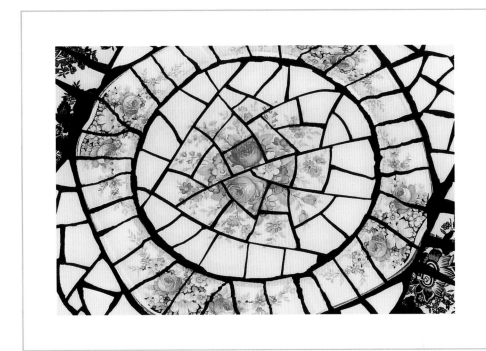

Nightstand

How can you use a square dish in your design?

I buy square plates whenever possible as they provide an alternate shape to work with. After all, you can only do so much with circles. In the nightstand, the border of a square plate is set on the diagonal around the center of a circular plate. The square shape provides the piece with some straight lines in the central design. The border from two large black transferware plates makes up the outside edge. The piece is grouted in black because a light-colored grout would not have been bold enough for the black nightstand. The continuity of the piece is maintained by the selection of china that has strong color in the floral pieces and black accents.

OPPOSITE: *If you find that as black grout cures, it has a hazy look to it, apply a very thin coat of light canola oil. Allow the oil to soak into the grout to restore the color to solid black. Using window cleaner and a soft cloth, wipe off any residual oil on the china.*

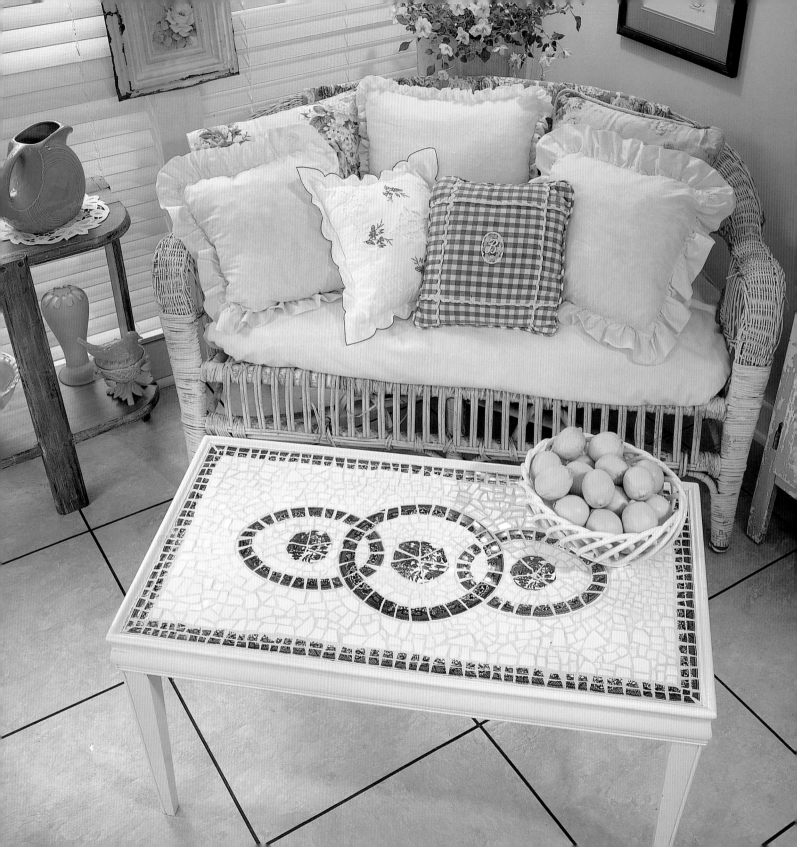

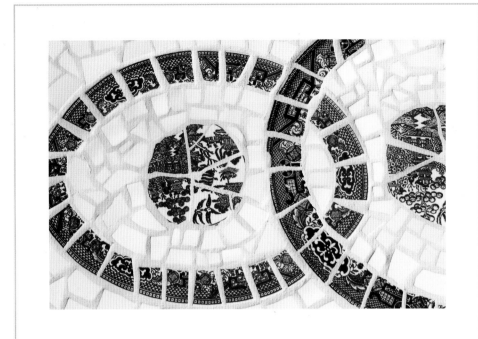

Blue Willow Coffee Table

What dish pattern is at home with any traditional decor?

Because of its theme, color, and design, Blue Willow is compatible with a variety of traditional decors. It is probably the most versatile of all china patterns and is so popular that there are actually Blue Willow conventions held annually throughout the United States. This pattern is readily available and relatively affordable. I like the pattern because it provides a bold color to work with. When paired with simple off-white china it results in a fresh and inviting piece, although its primary color of blue complements almost any floral pattern. Pieces cut from the pattern and placed in an organized design such as the center intertwining rings and the outside edge have a striking effect.

OPPOSITE: *This style of coffee table has a molding edge that perfectly frames a mosaic. Because this feature exists on the base, the mosaic could have been done without worrying about selecting finished border pieces for the outside edge. However, these border pieces were used anyway because they complement those in the central design and give the entire piece a more refined look.*

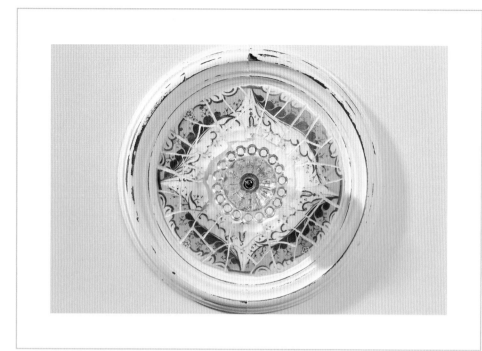

Dessert Buffet

ABOVE: *Since the door pulls are in the center of the mosaic, care must be taken to not cover up the screw holes with china. It is grouted normally. Before the grout dries, the screw holes must be cleared with a tool such as a Phillips screwdriver.*

To get the more refined look of unsanded grout, but also avoid the possibility that it might crack, mix sanded off-white grout with bright white unsanded grout in a 1:1 ratio.

How can you create a bold piece without using color?

bought this dessert buffet over two years ago because I knew the circular frames on each door were naturally suited for picasiette. I could have used a colorful floral plate inside these frames or I could have covered the entire door. Instead, I chose a very understated pair of gray-and-white porcelain plates.

When working with a design that has such an understated color combination, the details are critical. In this case, the antique glass door pulls became and integral part of the design. Notice how the gold backplate emphasizes the scalloped shape of the pulls and enhances the gold overlay painting of the plates.

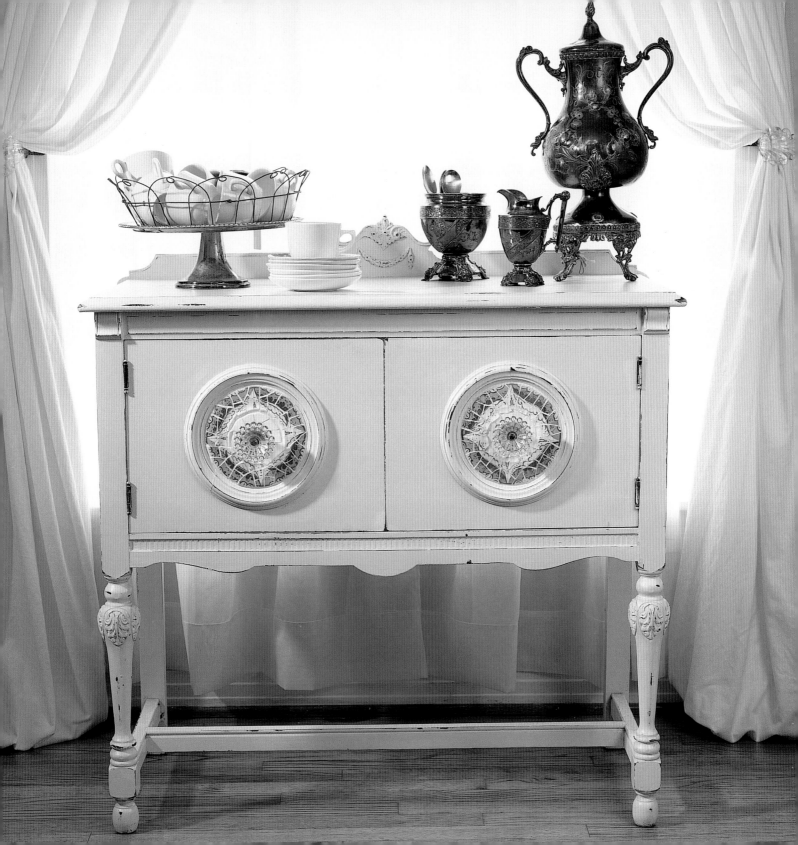

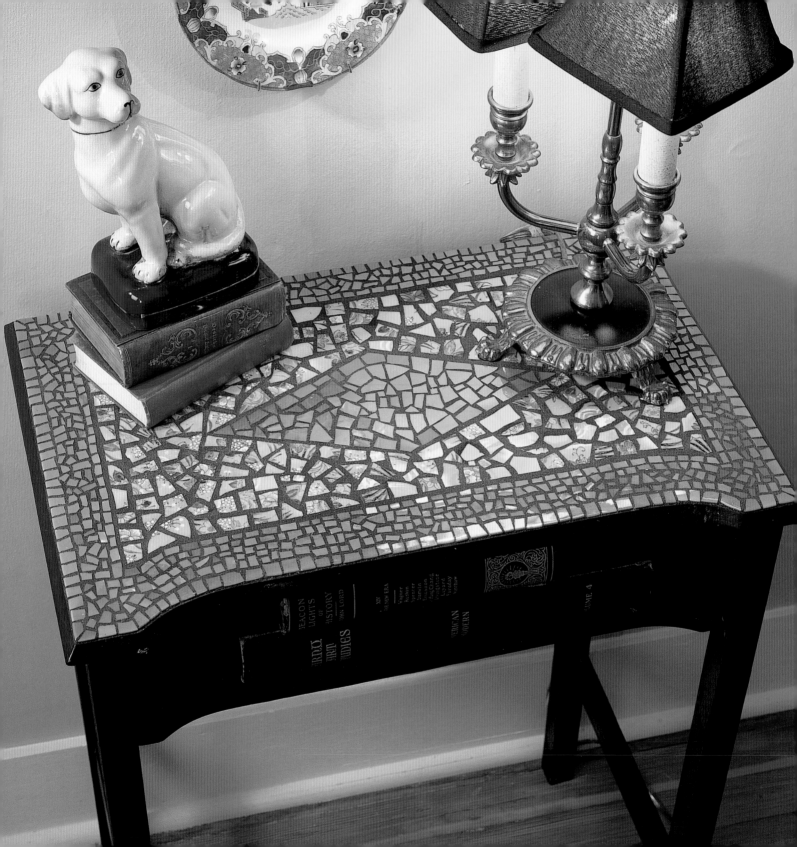

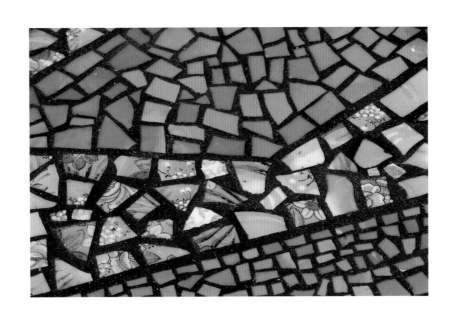

Hall Table

How can you use patterned china to fill in the field?

For this piece, I used colorful lusterware dishes in patterned amber and plain periwinkle. Normally, I use patterned china to make up the foreground design. However, for this hall table I decided that the periwinkle would do nicely to create a solid diamond in the center and a thick border around the edge of the piece. This left the patterned china to fill in the field. Each piece was positioned at random, leaving slightly larger grout joints than those allowed in the central and outside designs. This small detail provides even more contrast, giving a looser, unrestrained feeling to the field. Black grout sets off the jewel tones in the china.

ABOVE: *The central diamond design and the outside border on this table are created with pieces cut from periwinkle lusterware. It is helpful to position the pieces for the outer edges of these two elements, then fill in the design. Notice that the placement of pieces on the outside edge is somewhat uniform, but not entirely.*

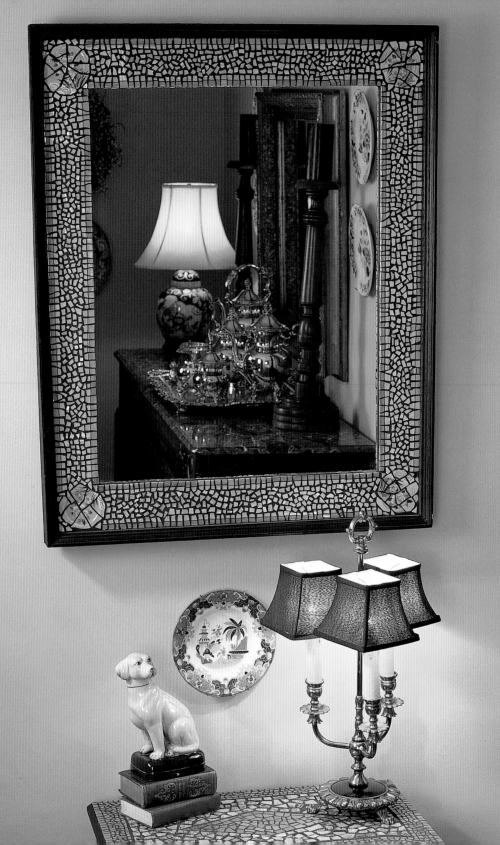

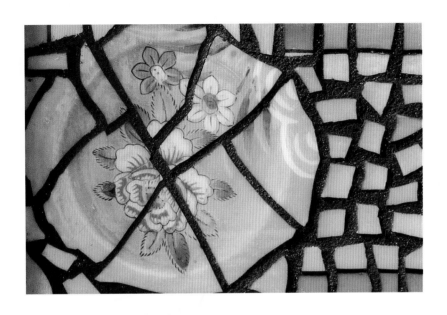

Hall Mirror

How can you make a mosaic to coordinate with one you already have?

picked up this basic frame at a yard sale, knowing that it would be perfect for holding a mirror above the Hall Table featured on page 83. Again, I used lusterware dishes but in a slightly different pattern and color scheme. Each of the four corners are anchored by a saucer center with a floral motif, surrounded by light celadon green in the frame's border. The common colors of periwinkle and amber included in the frame's border help to tie both the pieces together. As with the border on the table, it is helpful to construct the outer edges of the border, then fill in the center. Again, black grout is used to accentuate the colors in the design. The frame was painted black to match the Hall Table.

OPPOSITE: *Keep in mind whether or not your base can hold the weight of the finished mosaic. You may need to sure it up or add braces to help evenly distribute the weight.*

Paint the base first, then work the mosaic and grout it. You may then need to go back and touch up any painted sections that the grout has marred.

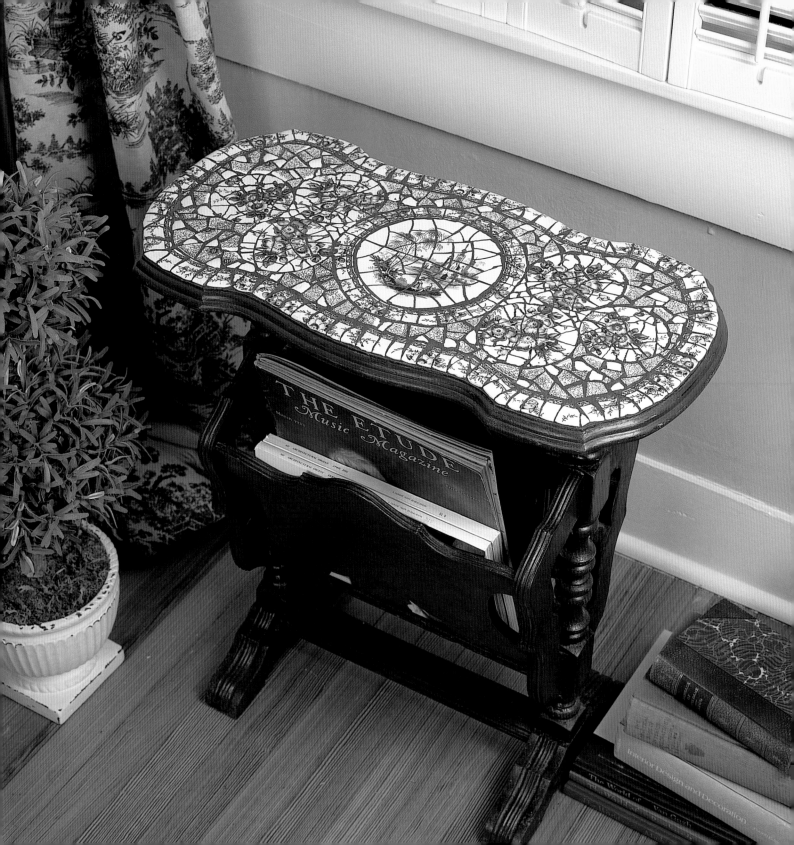

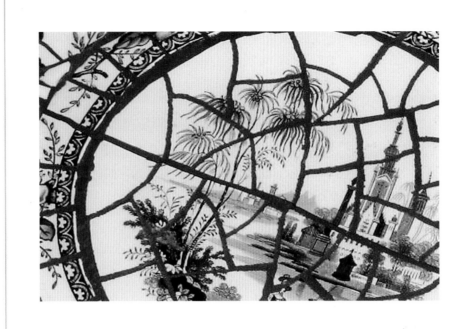

Magazine Stand

How can you frame your mosaic, using the furniture piece itself?

L ook for a piece that has a routed wooden edge. This type of edge creates a good frame for the mosaic. You can paint it the same color as the grout. Place the smooth-edged border pieces at the point where the flat part of the table begins, then work the central design.

This piece is the perfect combination of china, pattern, and furniture. Pieces of brown transferware are used for the large central design and to fill in the empty spaces between the three smaller floral-patterned plate centers at either side and the outside edge of the mosaic. Dark brown grout is used to complement the brown transferware.

OPPOSITE: *Often, when working with an old piece of furniture as the base for your mosaic, the piece will expand or contract and separate as time goes by, causing your mosaic to crack. If this happens, do not throw out the mosaic or worry about how to repair the furniture piece. Simply mix up more grout and fill in the cracks.*

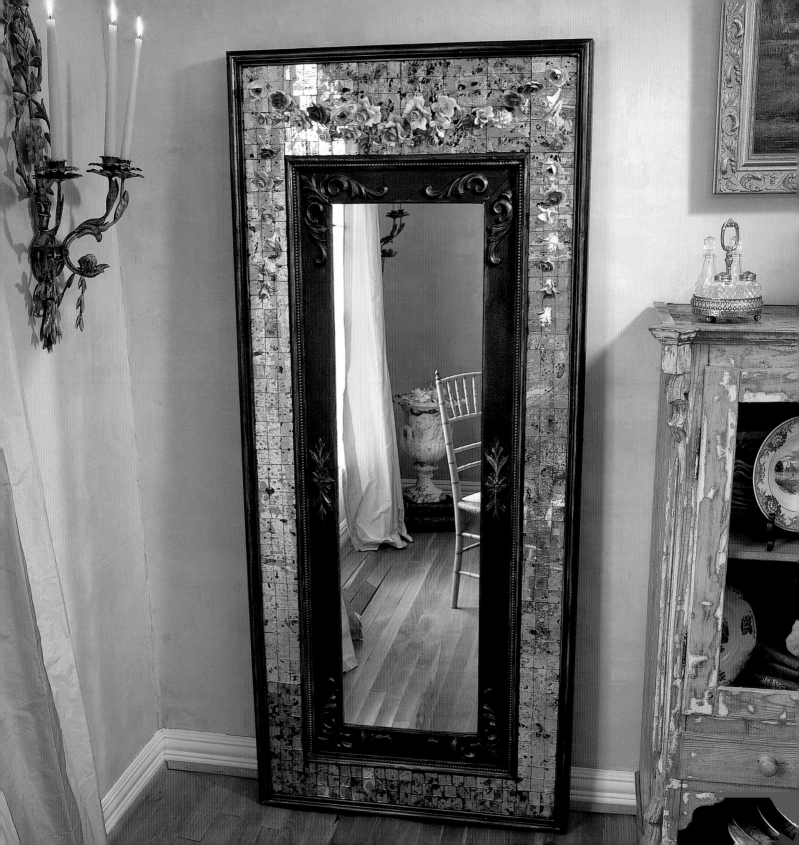

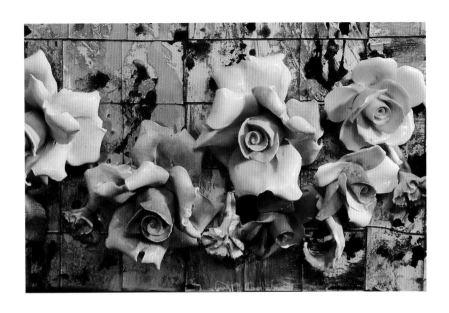

Victorian Door

How can you use an antique door as a base?

Antique doors can be easily found at flea markets and salvage yards, and they make a great start for stunning mosaic projects. Look for one that has a wide outside border for applying the mosaic and a glass window that can be replaced with a full-length mirror. One terrific feature that doors have is their ability to be taken off their hinges and laid flat so that you are not fighting against gravity as the mosaic is applied. I used hundreds of approximately 1"-square aged mirror pieces to cover the entire surface of the door (see Mirror Antiquing on page 36). Then I adhered vintage porcelain roses and flowers across the top to create a garland.

OPPOSITE: *In traditional tile mosaics, metallic tile, or Smalti, which is made by sandwiching gold or silver leaf between two thin pieces of glass, is often used to add reflective qualities to the piece. To get the look of Smalti, at a fraction of the cost, use the alternate instructions for antiquing a mirror (see page 39).*

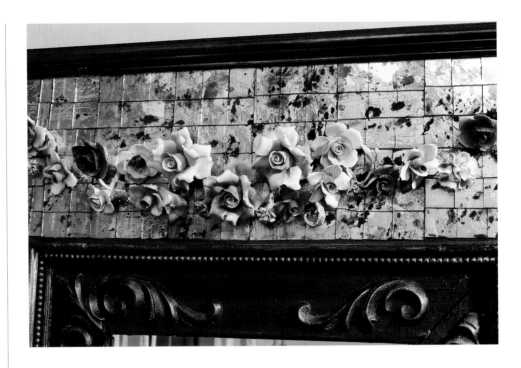

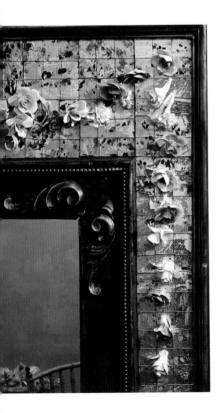

TECHNICAL DISCUSSION

Originally, this door had glass where the interior mirror is. I painted the entire piece black and used a mixture of clear paste wax and gold powder to highlight the high points of the carving and the molding.

I then antiqued about 15 12"-square mirror tiles, which are easily found in the bathroom department at your local hardware store. I measured the width of the side border and divided by three to determine what size to cut the mirror tiles. I used a glass cutter, following manufacturer's instructions, to cut the tiles. I made certain to antique a few extra pieces of mirror as there were bound to be a few miscuts.

The mirror pieces were quite easy to install with a very thin layer of tile mastic. Once dry, I used black unsanded grout to fill in the spaces between each tile. Since the spaces between each tile were so narrow, unsanded grout was necessary. I then adhered each porcelain flower onto the mirror with clear epoxy.

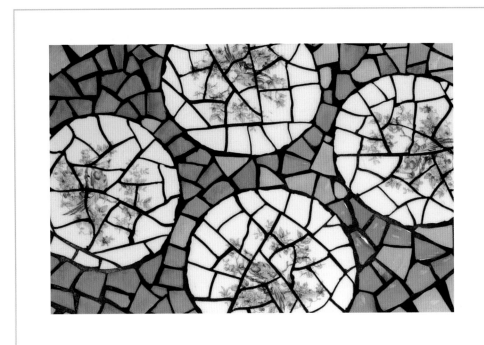

Oval Tea Table

How can you use colored lusterware with china?

For this piece, I paired periwinkle lusterware with a set of wonderful pheasant-patterned plates. They complement each other in both style and color. It is often difficult to find china patterns that are both colorful and sophisticated, but I find that Japanese lusterware—with its beautiful jewel-like colors and iridescent finish—fills this bill. It is commonly found in periwinkle blue, amber gold, and a light celadon green. I chose to use two shades of periwinkle to create the inner border and to fill in the field. Lusterware is most often found in cups, saucers, and dessert plates because it was a very popular finish to use for tea services.

ABOVE: *Shown from above, the design for this table is made up of four pheasant-patterned plates set on a field of periwinkle lusterware and finished with a pheasant-patterned edge. Notice the uniform effect achieved by maintaining a similar distance between the plates and centering them in this oval design.*

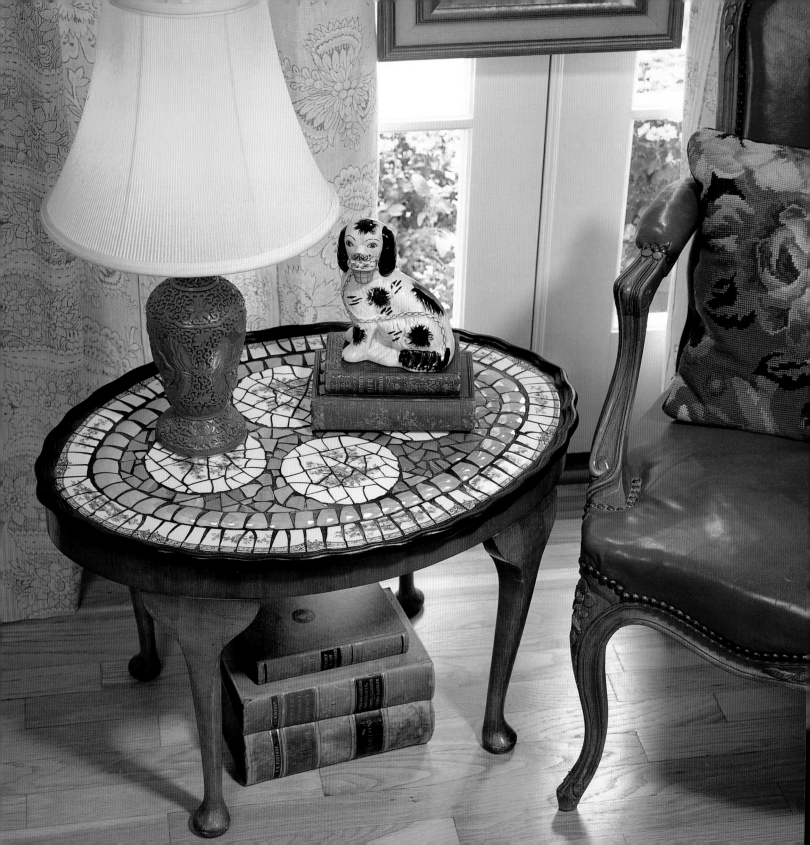

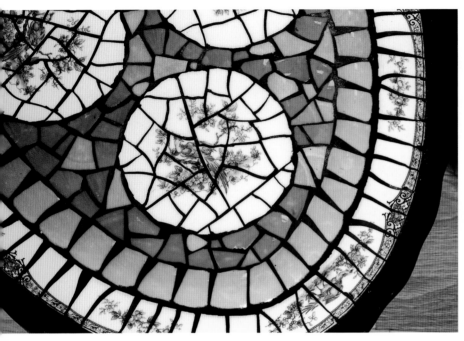

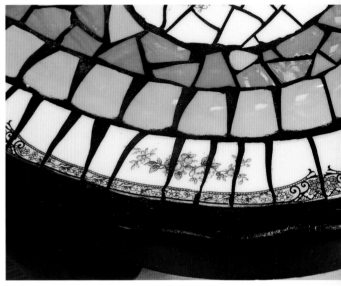

TECHNICAL DISCUSSION

It is very common to find side and coffee tables that have a frame around their outside edge. They were originally designed to accommodate a piece of protective glass. These table-tops make great surfaces for picasiette. Their design renders it unnecessary to pay close attention to how the edge of your mosaic is finished. You do not have to worry about finding smooth plate edges or struggling with the alignment. However, you may find that using a continuous border will add definition to your project.

ABOVE LEFT & ABOVE RIGHT: *Notice the placement of the china pieces around the outside of the table. The outside edge border was cut from the same plates as the central motifs. An inner border was created with pieces cut from saucers in a lighter shade of periwinkle blue. Lusterware has the unusual characteristic of being glazed, or colored, on the front and back of the piece, allowing you to use either side according to your design. The saucer pieces were placed with the back side up to create a smoother border.*

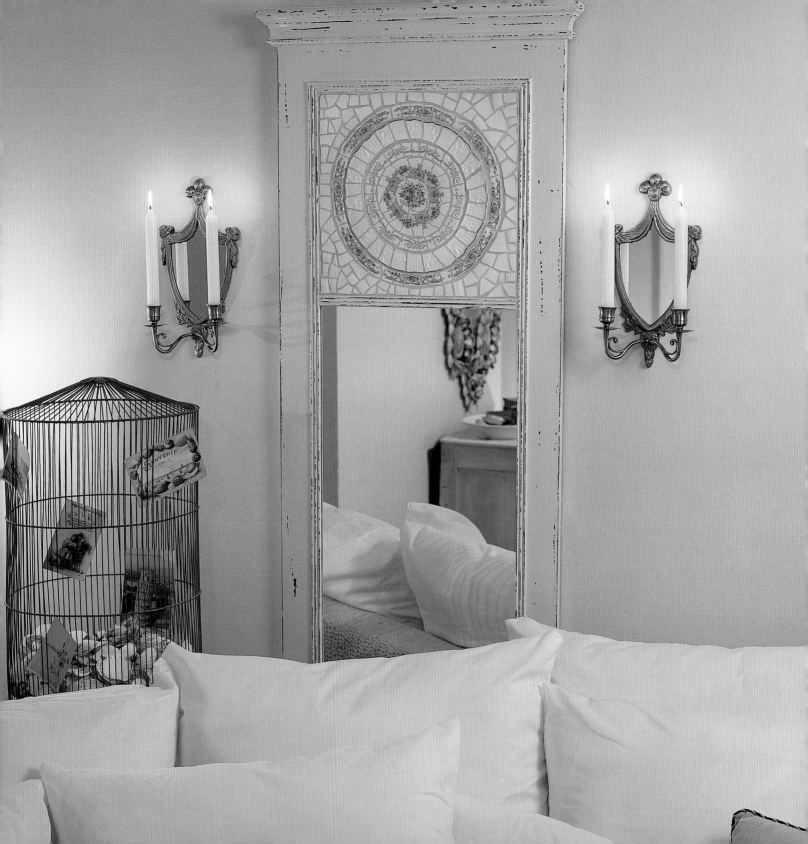

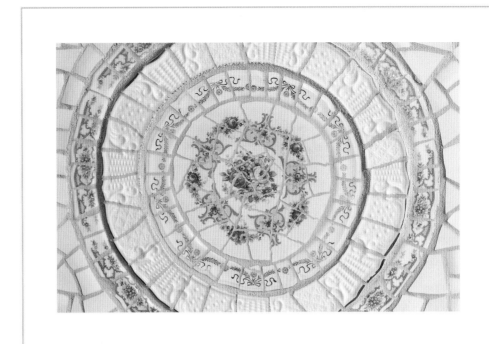

China Trumeau Mirror

How can you borrow an idea from a classical design?

This style of mirror is called a trumeau mirror. Trumeau is a French word that refers to something in three parts. In traditional antique trumeau mirrors, you would usually find a painted landscape scene in the top third, and mirror in the bottom two-thirds. In this case, I used the top third for mosaics instead.

This open panel requires a floral dinner plate for the center and the outer ring, a gilded dessert plate edge for the inner ring, and plenty of off-white china for the field. Begin at the center and work outward. Use tile mastic to adhere the pieces onto the panel and grout as usual.

ABOVE: *All off-white china is not necessarily the same. Try to pull from the same set of plates when designing a piece.*

When shopping for china, you may find a pattern that you would never want to use in any design. Instead of simply passing it by, keep in mind that if you turn the plate over, the back may be a great source for off-white china—perfect for filling in the field of a mosaic.

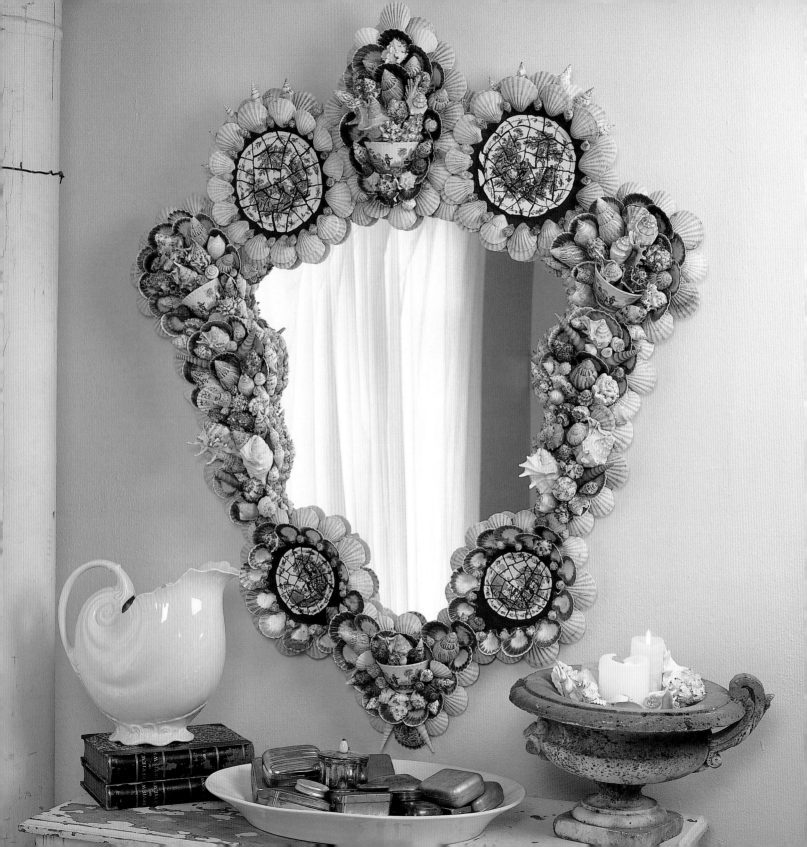

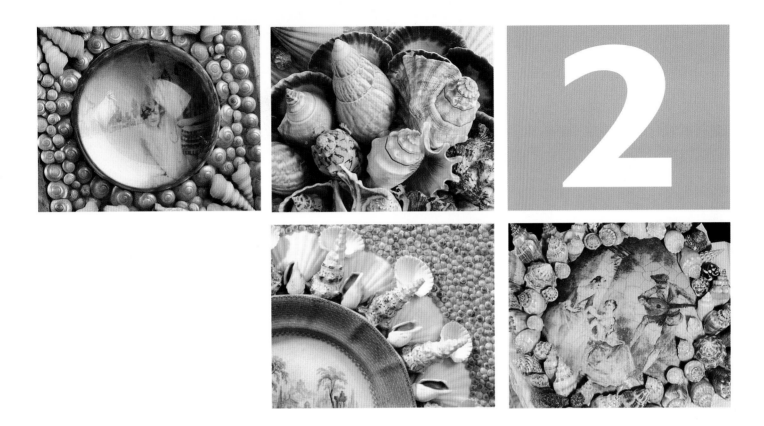

Shellwork

ONE OF THE JOYS of shellwork mosaics is that you are using natural works of art and architectural wonders in your own creations. Frank Lloyd Wright is said to have described shells as "Such greatness with such simplicity." It seems that shells never go out of style. Although their popularity has peaked at different times throughout history, the use of shells has been documented as far back as the 1500s. Marine motifs in all styles were wildly popular in Italy and France in the 16th and 17th centuries. At that time, shell collection and shellwork was the hobby of the aristocracy. European nobility was inspired by shell mosaics found in places like the Medici's Boboli Gardens in Florence and at the Villa d'Este outside Rome. They eagerly commissioned artists to re-create these marvels on their own estates.

OPPOSITE: *The Shellwork & Transferware Mirror on pages 119–121 is a wonderful example of what can be done with a combination of picasiette and shellwork.*

ABOVE: *These photos show close-up details of several shellwork projects that are presented on the following pages.*

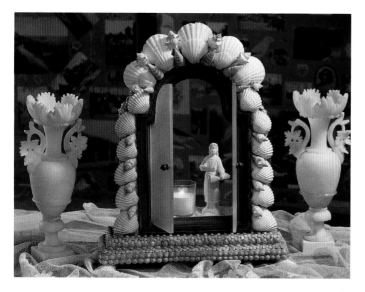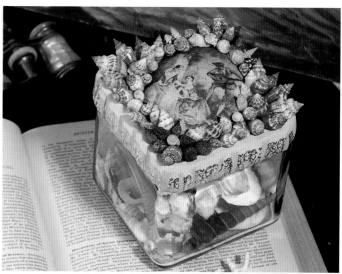

ABOVE LEFT: *The Frame Altar on pages 116–118 is an excellent example of the way shells can be used to enhance decor and provide a feeling of luxury.*

ABOVE RIGHT: *Although small in size, the Collector's Box on pages 114–115 is an example of the range of colors that can be found in shells and used on one piece.*

A favorite representation was the incorporation of grotto-style shellwork into the architectural embellishments of outside buildings.

Shellwork and collection once again became popular with Victorian women for use in home decor in the 18th century. Shells were used to create intricate compositions that resembled flowers, hearts, and geometric patterns. These works of art were usually mounted behind glass inside a hinged, two-sided wooden box. Legend has it that home-sick sailors first created these boxes, called Sailor's valentines, as gifts for their loved ones and sweethearts during idle hours aboard ship.

Shellwork reemerged in both the United States and Europe during the 1940s and now at the turn of the 21st century, it is back once again.

Because shells have a certain intrigue and mystery about them, I have always admired them in their natural state as well as in vintage shellwork pieces. I lived several years in New England while attending college and spent a lot of time on the beach. I came home to Texas with several boxes of shells. My mother tactfully suggested that perhaps I did not need so many shells, but I could not bear to part with even one of them. Each one represented a memory, a stroll along the coast, or a picnic on the beach.

Over the years, I amassed an impressive assortment of shells, but was not certain what to do with them. I have learned that the difference between collectors and hoarders is that collectors use or prominently display their shells while hoarders pile them in cardboard boxes hoping to someday get around to doing something with them.

For years, I entertained thoughts of combining shellwork with picasiette before I attempted my first project. That first project marked my transition from chipped-china mosaics to shellwork as my primary design focus. Working with shells has proven to be both rewarding and challenging.

COLORATION OF SHELLS

When working with shells, you will find certain limitations regarding color and structure. The color palette of shells is fairly limited. The predominant color of most shells is brown. However, if you look closely, you will find natural hues of indigo blue, violet, and coral scattered throughout most shells. Shells are like flowers—no matter how many colors are in one flower or how many different flowers you choose to put together, you can be certain that the colors will always complement each other.

Also, there are a several ways to manipulate the colors of the shells:

Paint—If you want a specific color, you can always paint the shells. Using spray enamel limits your color choices but provides for ease of application. Flat paint and shades of black, white, and cream are always safe choices. You might also consider gold or silver for a dramatic, more formal effect.

Fabric Dye—Fabric dye, available at your grocery store, offers an array of bold color choices. Dilute the dye and apply to each shell with a paintbrush. Because shell surfaces and dye intensity vary, you may find that the dye may rub off once it is dry. If this occurs, apply a topcoat of polyurethane sealer. Dyeing works best for light-colored porous shells.

Wood Stain—Applying wood stains to your shells once a project is complete can give a unifying effect. Although most stains are in brown tones, color-washing your entire project with a single color pulls everything together.

Gesso—Gesso is a product used to prepare a canvas for painting. It is available at art supply stores and craft stores. It is a thick white liquid that can be applied to shells with a paintbrush. It leaves behind a hazy, chalky film. Gesso is not opaque enough to entirely change the color of a shell without applying several coats; but by applying just one or two coats, you can tone down the natural color of the shell.

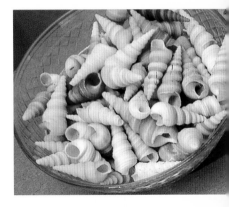

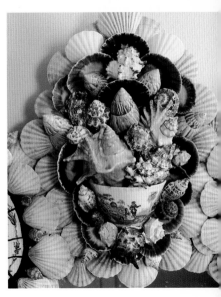

ABOVE: *Shells are typically available in a limited color palette made up of shades of brown. However, upon close inspection, you will usually find some natural hues of indigo blue, violet, and coral as well.*

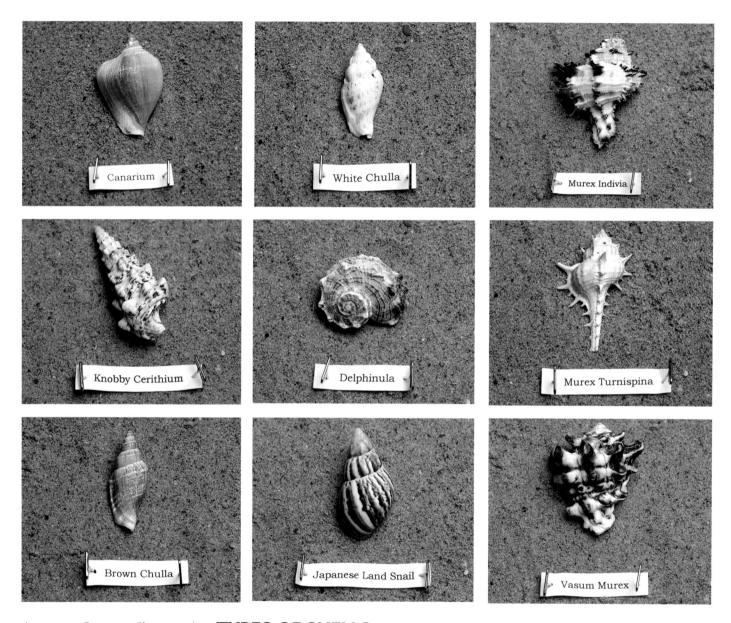

Canarium	White Chulla	Murex Indivia
Knobby Cerithium	Delphinula	Murex Turnispina
Brown Chulla	Japanese Land Snail	Vasum Murex

ABOVE AND OPPOSITE: *Shown here are various species of shells.*

TYPES OF SHELLS

There are many species of shells from which to choose when you are planning a shell-work design. Those shown above are the ones that I have used most in the projects in this book. I find that it is best to have a large selection at hand when you are actually working on

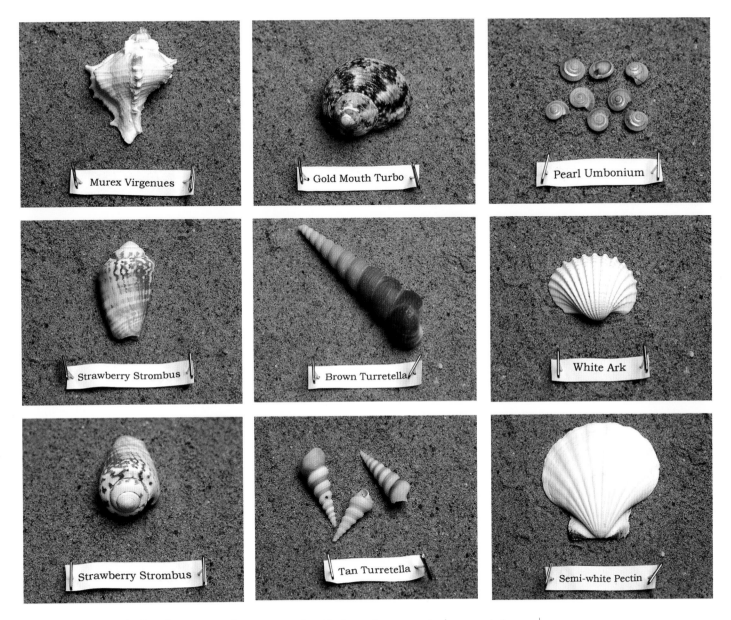

the project. Most shells fall into one of two categories: 1) those that are univalve, consisting of one spiraling piece, like the chulla and the murex; and 2) those that are bivalve, or made up of two connecting pieces, like the pectin. Be aware that shells naturally only grow in one direction. This makes creating a symmetrical or mirrored design somewhat challenging.

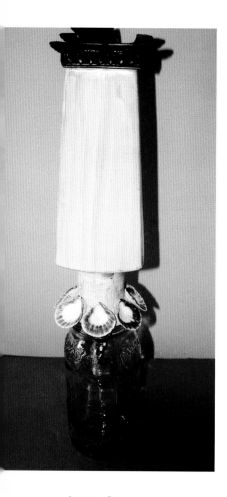

DESIGNING WITH SHELLS

The basic design principles that I have presented regarding picasiette mosaics will pertain to shellwork mosaics with equal importance. Taking the time to plan your design and making certain you have enough materials to execute it is the key to a successful project.

Actually, I must admit it seems like no matter what you do with shells, the project turns out to be a success. Because of their wonderful natural beauty it is hard to mess them up. A very rustic, disorganized pattern can sometimes be just as aesthetically pleasing as a formal, more structured one.

APPLYING SHELLS

When I begin a shellwork piece, I generally lay the base flat and begin positioning the shells to see what kind of repetitive pattern I can come up with. This process can become very tricky because the shells are often rounded and tend to roll around on the surface. However, it is definitely worth taking the time to get a feel for where the design is going before you start using adhesives.

As it often is in life, your greatest enemy in shellwork is gravity. Since the finished project will probably have vertical surfaces, you must think of creative ways to make those surfaces horizontal until the adhesive is dry. Sometimes this can be as simple as turning the piece on its side. However, in some cases it can be quite a challenge. For example, the Lamp on pages 108–109 had to be turned upside down and set inside the mouth of a large jar so that the shell layers could be built up while they were drying. You must take the time to let one layer dry so that it can support the next layer.

WORKING A SHELLWORK PROJECT

Shellwork projects require a lot of planning just as picasiette projects do. However, shells are not as predictable as are broken china pieces. With shells, you must take what you get because you cannot control the their size and shape. Therefore, you must be flexible in your design and have a lot of shells available to choose from.

For the Memory Box project on pages 106–107, I determined in advance that I would use a dome-shaped glass paperweight over a vintage photo as my centerpiece and surround it with two borders of umbonium shells.

Materials

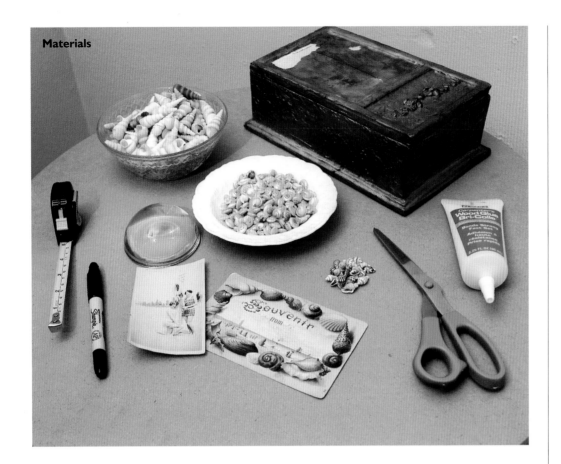

**Materials needed
to apply the design:**

- Assorted shells
- Found object: dome-
  shaped glass paper
  weight
- Permanent marking pen
- Photocopies of artwork
- Scissors
- Tape measure
- Tweezers (not shown)
- Wood glue
- Wooden box for base

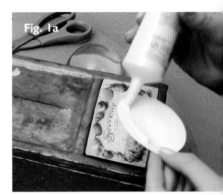

Fig. 1a

INSTRUCTIONS

Lay out all of your materials in one spot, making certain you have plenty of
different shells from which to choose. Because of the size of the project, I
selected small shells to work with. If this were a large-scale project I would
recommend having baskets of larger shells available.

STEP 1

Cut out a color copy of a vintage postcard and a vintage photograph to fit
under the dome-shaped glass paperweight. Adhere both pieces onto the
box lid with wood glue. (Figs. 1a–1b)

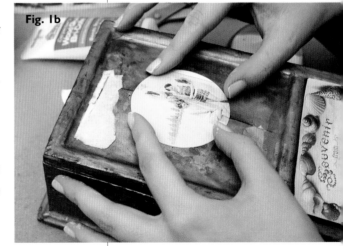

Fig. 1b

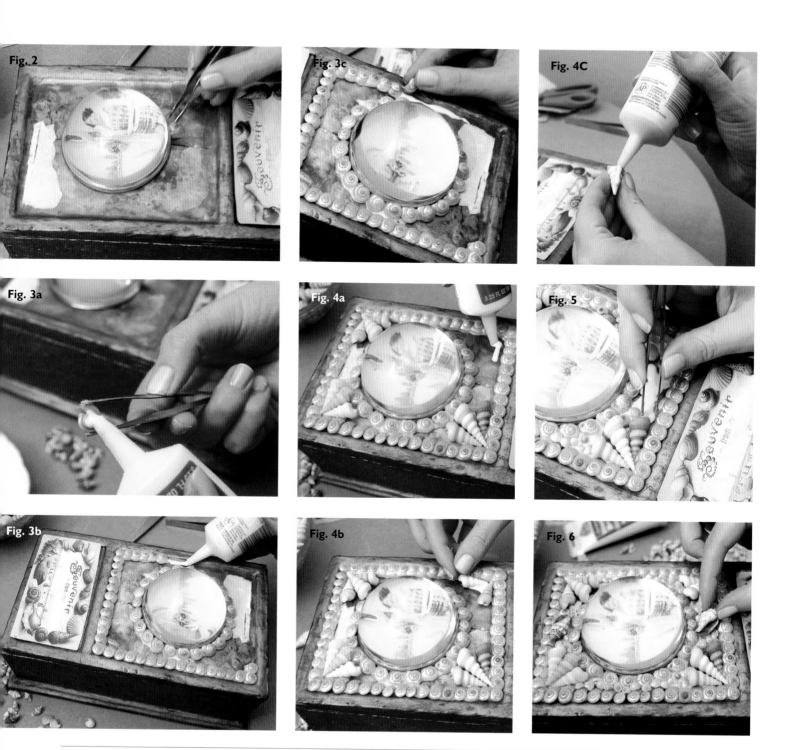

Fig. 2

Fig. 3c

Fig. 4C

Fig. 3a

Fig. 4a

Fig. 5

Fig. 3b

Fig. 4b

Fig. 6

STEP 2

Secure the dome-shaped glass paperweight onto the box lid with clear silicone or epoxy. (Fig. 2)

STEP 3

Using a thick wood glue and tweezers if desired, adhere the umbonium shell borders around the paperweight and the outside edge of the box lid. (Figs. 3a–3c)

STEP 4

Try several different shell shapes and configurations for the corners. Carefully select a collection of shells for each corner that fills up the entire space—a grouping of turretella shells works nicely. (Figs. 4a–4c)

STEP 5

Once the borders and corners are complete, it is just a matter of filling in the field. Use a smaller version of the silver umbonium shells that were used on the outside edges. (Fig. 5)

STEP 6

If you feel the top and bottom still need a little something extra to provide balance, add two similarly sized chullas. Turn them upside down so that the coral peeking out of the inside of the shell will complement the corals in the postcard. (Fig. 6)

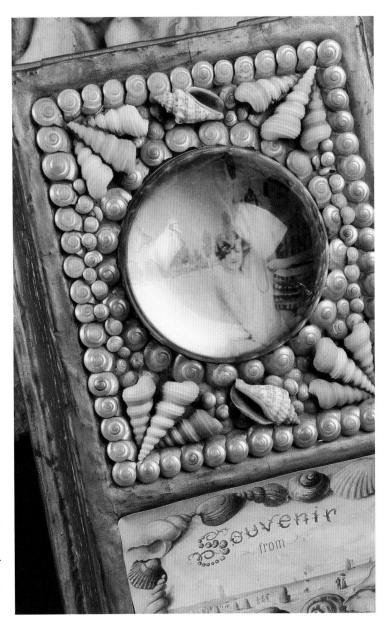

ABOVE: *This close-up of the Memory Box on pages 106–107 shows how the coral color inside chulla shells coordinates with the color on the postcard.*

Note: For most shellwork projects, you will use either white craft glue or wood glue to adhere the shells onto the base. These glues are quite strong and stand the test of time. If you are trying to place a heavier shell, try using clear silicone or epoxy.

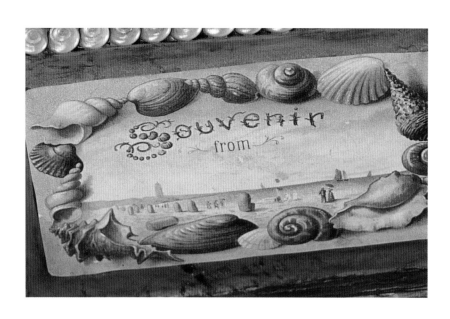

Memory Box

OPPOSITE: *If you cannot find a domed paperweight, simply have a flat piece of glass cut that covers your photograph. This will result in a slightly different finished piece, but still cover your photograph and protect it from shellwork gluing.*

How can you use photographs in a shellwork mosaic?

I have an obsession for clear glass paperweights. Open any drawer in my house and you are likely to come across one or two tucked away in a corner. This domed one was perfect to place over a vintage photograph of bathing beauties. Umbonium shells outline the paperweight and the edge of the box lid. Turretella shells are set in groups of three at each corner with one chulla shell above and below the paperweight. Umbonium shells are used to fill in the field. The postcard, a gift from a dear friend, arrived just in time to provide a colorful finishing touch to this memory box.

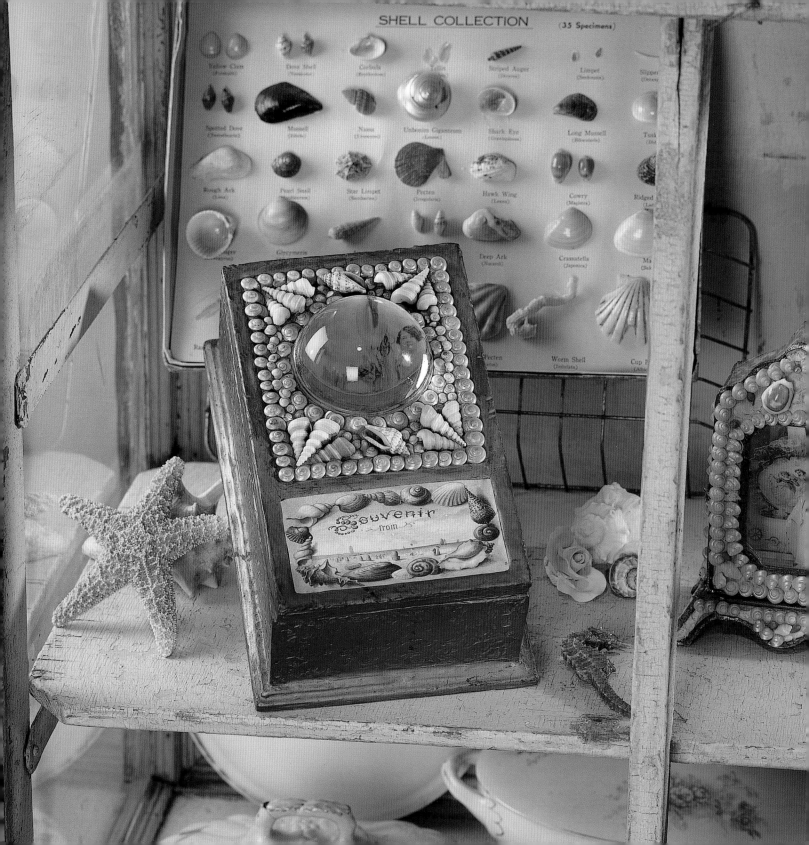

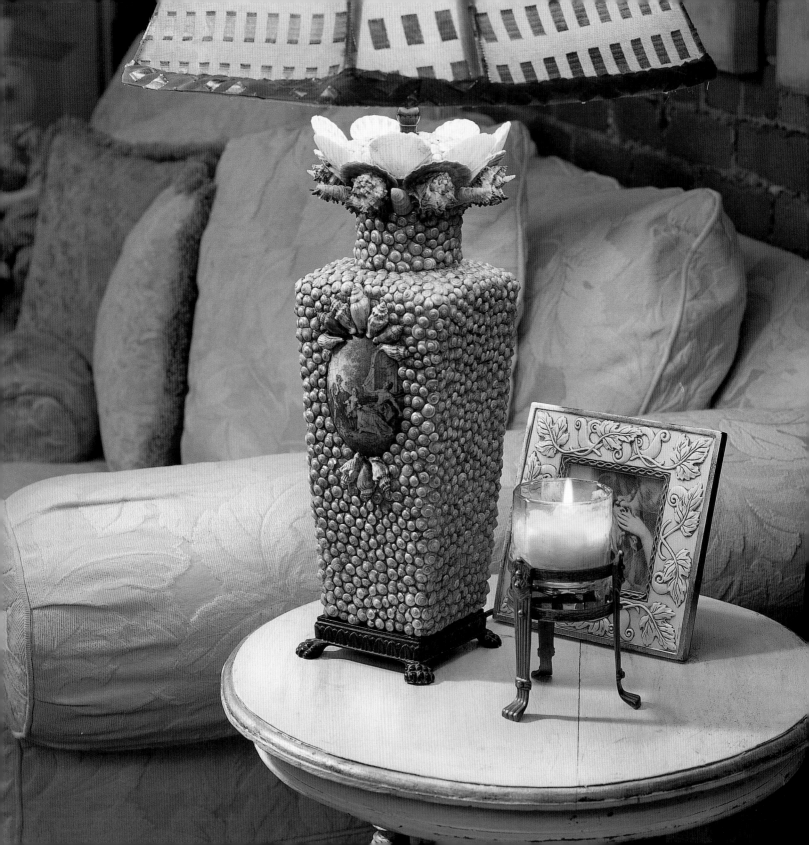

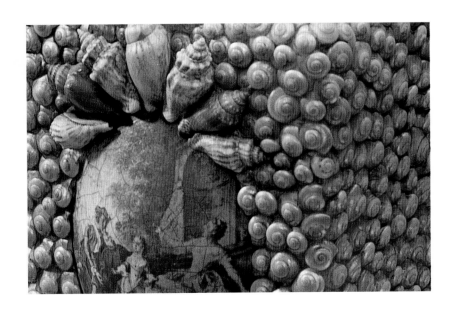

Lamp

How can you cover a vertical surface with shells?

A lamp is another one of those easy yard-sale finds that makes an excellent base for shellwork and mosaics. Because it is a vertical item, it must be laid on its side so that the shellwork can be done one section at a time.

The plaster medallions were in my collection of "things I might want to glue on something someday." They were just the right size and shape and inspired the entire design. They are accentuated at the top and bottom by brown chulla shells. The top rim is crowned with alternating semi-white pectin, tan turretella, and murex indivia shells. The majority of the base is covered with umbonium shells.

OPPOSITE: *The original surface of this lamp was a very dark color. Because the selected shells are light in color, the lamp is painted off-white before applying the shellwork. Any spaces that might show through between the shells, are complementary and almost unnoticeable.*

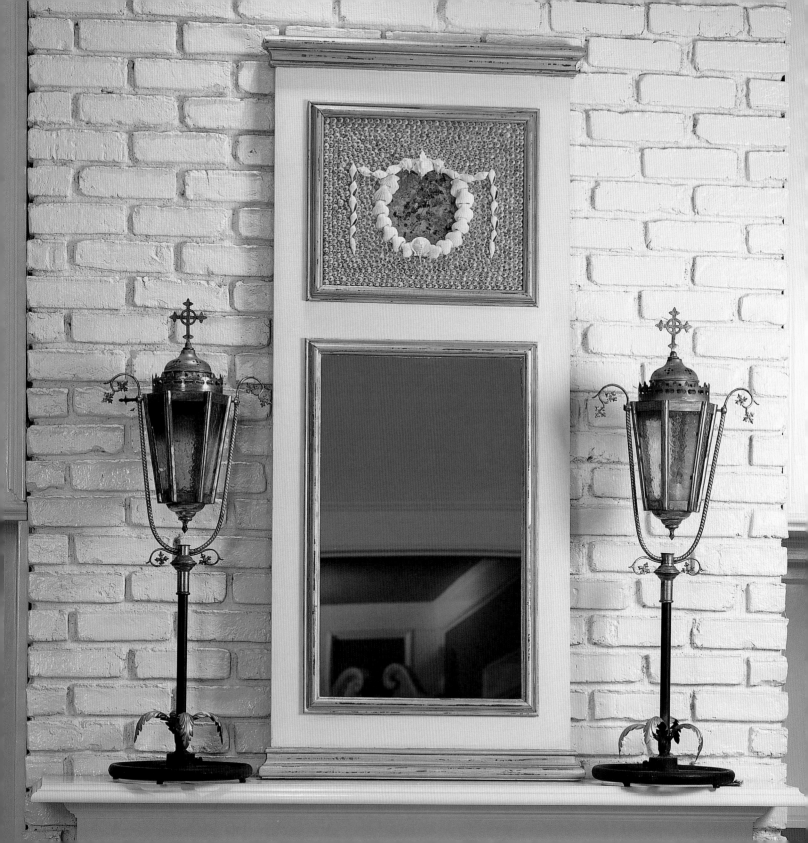

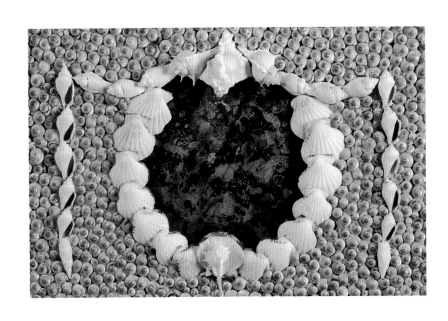

Frieze Trumeau Mirror

How can you use shells to imitate architectural elements?

This trumeau mirror is another example of the use of an antiqued mirror (see Mirror Antiquing on page 36). After aging a round mirror, which I purchased precut from a craft store, I used semi-white pectin and white chulla shells to fashion a wreath and garland around the mirror. I carefully selected shells that were as close to white as possible because I wanted them to resemble a plaster frieze. Once all of these shells were in place, I used pearl umbonium shells to outline the frieze design and fill in the field. Although umbonium shells are relatively plain, they are a pleasure to work with because they are available in a variety of sizes and fit easily next to each other.

ABOVE: *Notice that the chulla shells along each side have been turned so the inside is showing as opposed to the those that make up the swag. Keep in mind that there are different sides to the shells and different colors as well that you can use in your design.*

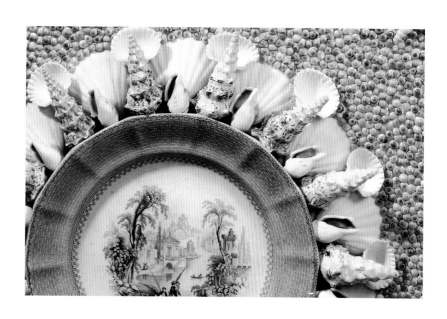

Shellwork & Transferware Screen

How can you use an unbroken dish in your shellwork design?

An antique dealer friend of mine brought this blue transferware plate home from a buying trip in New England. When I saw it, I knew that the soft blue would blend beautifully with the light-colored shells I had in mind for this antique fireplace screen. First, the dish is centered and adhered onto the fireplace screen with epoxy. Semi-white pectin, white ark, knobby cerithium, and white chulla shells are then carefully tucked in under the raised lip of the plate, creating a radiating effect. Each corner is embellished with a white ark and four turretella shells. Umbonium shells are used to fill in the field.

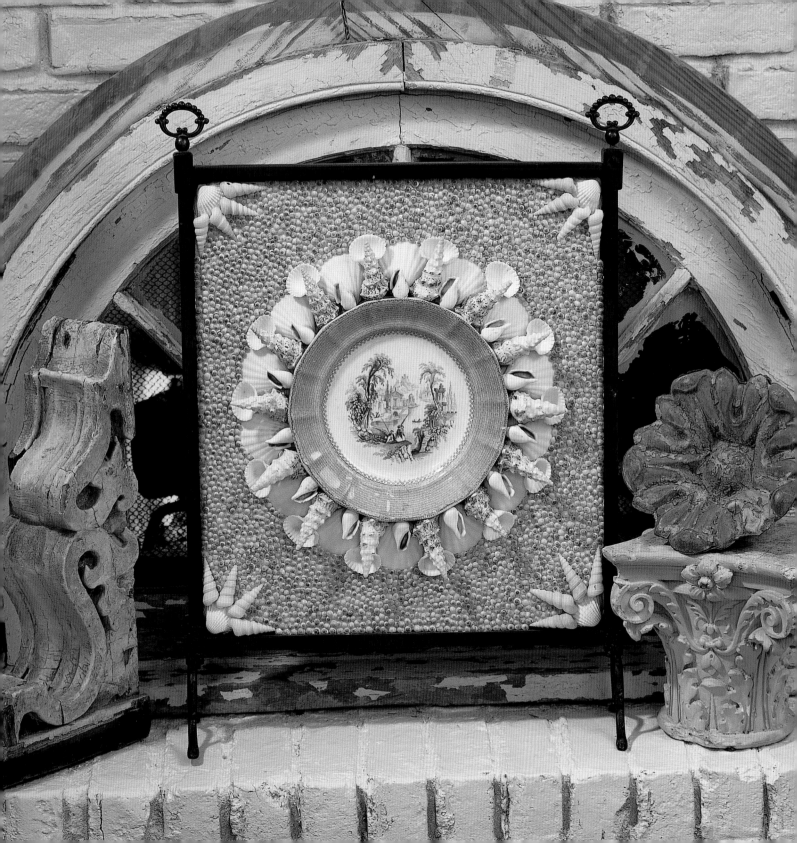

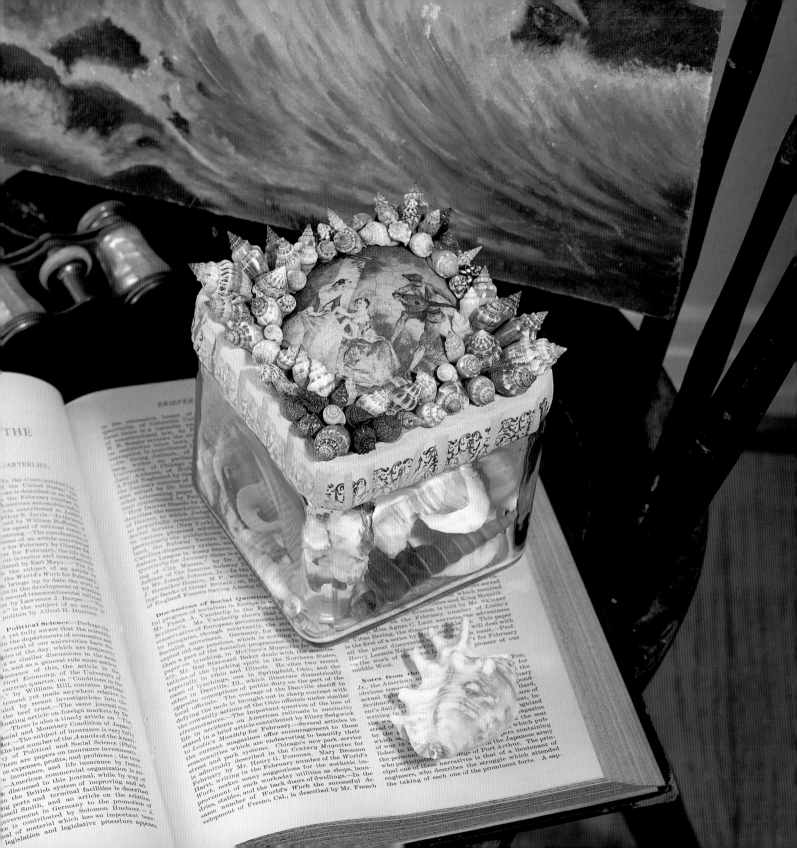

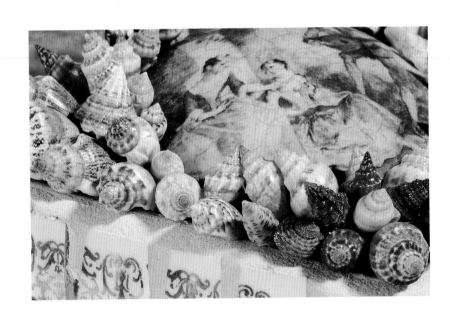

Collector's Box

How can you combine picasiette with shellwork?

Select a base that is small and a design that is simple. This is a fun little project that incorporates both. I used a square glass canister that can be found inexpensively at most discount stores. The edge of the lid is covered with a plate border adhered with mastic and grouted in the usual manner. This must be done before adhering the shell-work design on the top as the shells hang over the edge. I used a vintage plaster medallion for the centerpiece of the lid, but you could also use more shells, a photograph, or even a small mirror. Once the medallion is in position, tiny brown chulla shells are placed around it and around the edge of the lid. Finally, they are used to fill in the open spaces.

OPPOSITE: *Find a few close-up photographs of collectible shell-work. There are several fine gallery books that approach the subject that will give you a jump-start on how to design your own piece—working with the "masters" will increase your confidence and inspire your creativity.*

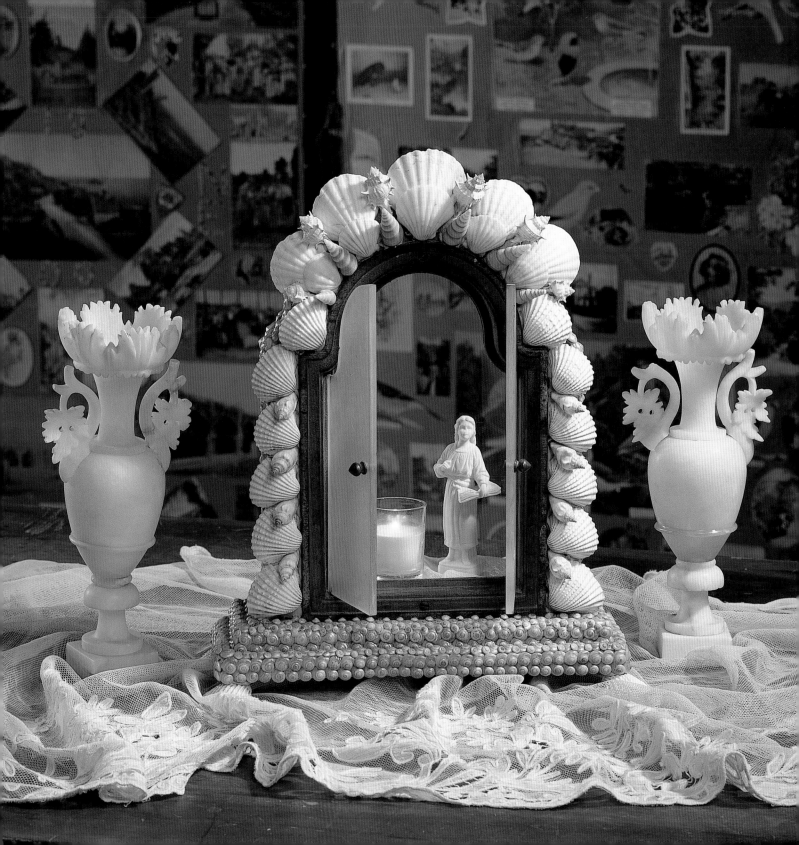

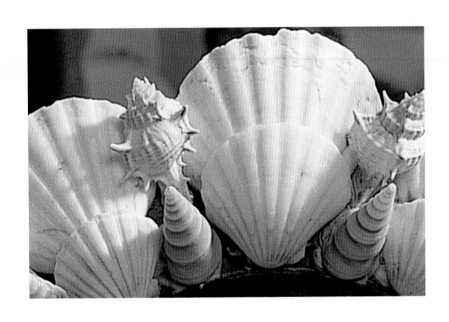

Frame Altar

How can you use a found item as a base for your design?

The base of this piece is a glass and brass spy window from a vintage door. It was just one of those things that I could not leave on the flea-market table. I took it home and did not think about it for months until one day I became inspired to turn it into an altar. I built up the base and sides with MDF and hardboard to provide a surface for placing layered pectin shells, turretella shells, and murex turnispina shells around the arch. I even used four carefully selected white ark shells to create dainty matching feet. Umbonium shells cover the tiered base to complete the tiny altar. It has become one of my favorite pieces.

ABOVE: *With a few simple modifications, an unlikely found item makes a unique base for a shellwork mosaic. Clock cases such as those found on mantle clocks and grandfather clocks are readily found in second-hand shops. These items can also be built up with MDF and covered with shells.*

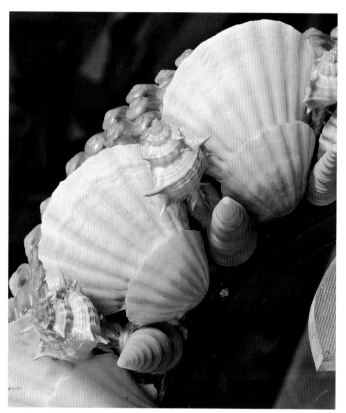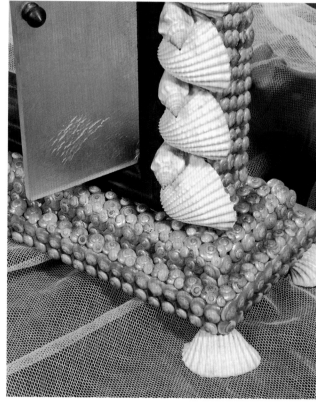

ABOVE LEFT: *Placement of the large semi-white pectin shells on the spy-door frame provides the foundation for the rest of the design. The smaller shells are adhered onto the base of their larger counterparts. Tan turretella and murex turnispina shells are used to fill in the gaps between the semi-white pectin shells.*

ABOVE RIGHT: *Here, you can see how white ark shells are used at each corner of the MDF base. They act as natural feet for the piece. These four shells must be of similar size and shape so the piece will sit squarely.*

TECHNICAL DISCUSSION

In order to start designing this piece, I laid the brass frame flat on a piece of craft paper and arranged shells around it in an appealing pattern. I then drew the outline around the shells. I used this as a template to create a border that surrounded the outside of the brass frame. To cut the ¼" hardboard that surrounds the top and sides, I used a jigsaw. The two-tiered base is made from ⅜" MDF, which you can have cut at your local hardware store.

Instead of using just one large semi-white pectin shell, I layered one small shell over a medium shell to create more texture. I also added four shells at each corner of the bottom of the base. This small detail added a great deal of character and interest.

All of the shells were adhered with mastic except the for the umbonium along the tiered base, which were adhered with gel wood glue.

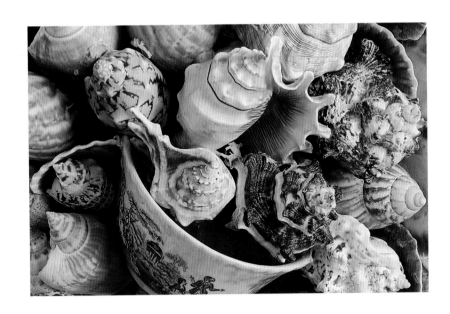

Shellwork & Transferware Mirror

How can you combine large areas of picasiette with shellwork?

The frame for this mirror was originally going to be designed for a chipped-china mosaic—without a single thought of incorporating shells. However, I did not get around to finishing the project, and the frame sat in the corner of my studio for more than two years collecting spiderwebs. One day I became inspired to create a piece that combined both picasiette and shellwork. This mirror, comprised of various shells and transferware plates and cups, was the exciting result. The broken plates are adhered onto the frame first. Then the shells are positioned around the transferware. Notice the special attention given to making certain the designs were mirrored from the left side to the right side.

OPPOSITE: *Shellwork design is much like floral design in that you are placing colors and shapes or groupings of the two to create balance, symmetry, and visual impact.*

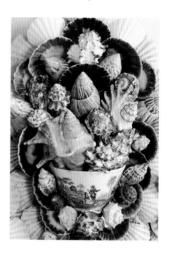

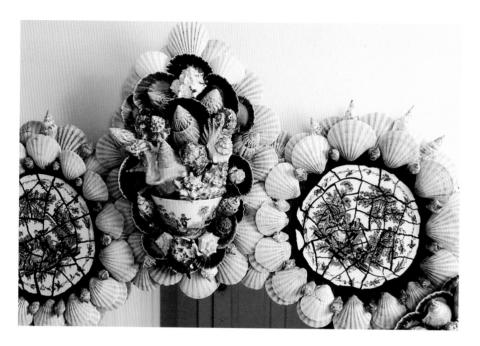

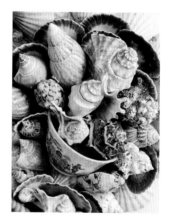

ABOVE: *Like-sized shells are placed in and around the teacups in a fanlike design to echo the fanning of the pectin shells. Some are facing outward while others are positioned facing in.*

TECHNICAL DISCUSSION

This project required a lot of planning. There are eight different design groupings symmetrically distributed throughout this piece, three across the top, one on each side, and three across the bottom. I first adhered the four plates with mastic. Then I installed the mirror (see Mirror Installation on pages 40–41). Next, I created borders for each design group with scalloped pectin shells. The center top, bottom, and sides were filled in with clusters of nestled shells adhered with clear silicone.

The grouting on this project was a little tricky since grout tends to get trapped in the shells. I did not want to get grout on the shells surrounding the plates, so I had to get a little creative. I bought a plastic diner-style ketchup bottle with a pointed funnel top. I mixed the grout with more water than usual so that it would be thin enough to be squeezed through the funnel. I carefully placed the grout around the shells so that it just settled into the shells without a lot of excess to clean up. Using the normal process, I applied enough grout to fill in the gaps around the plates.

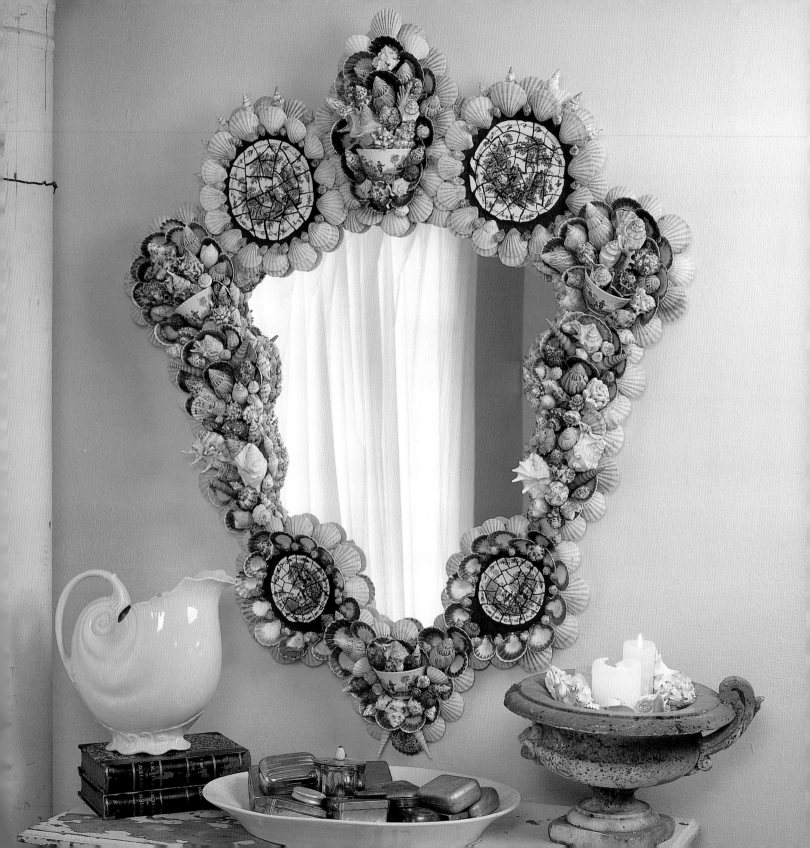

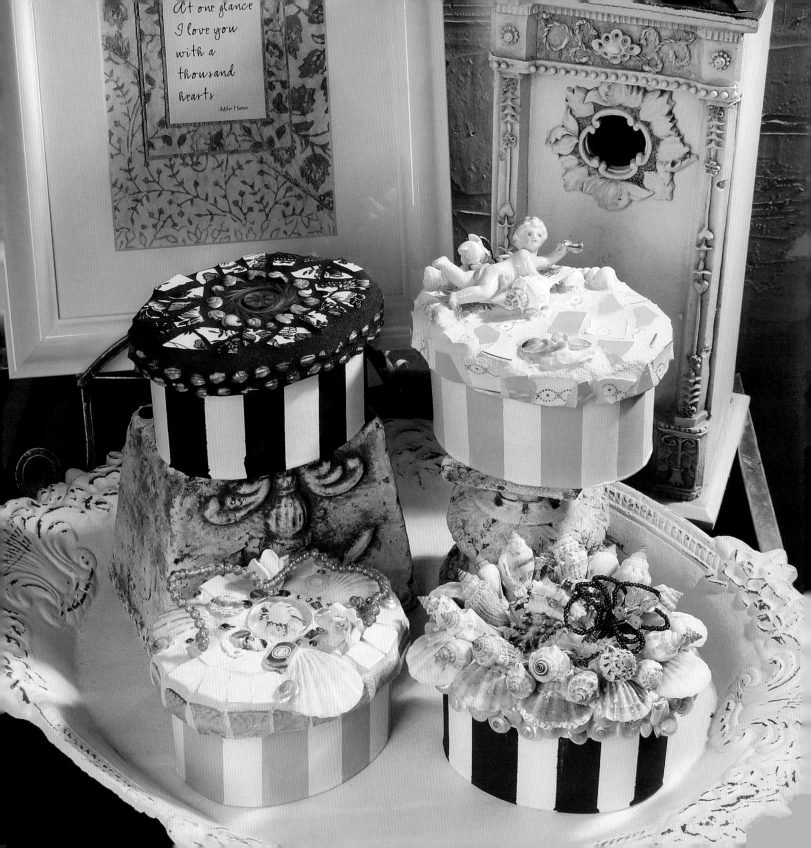

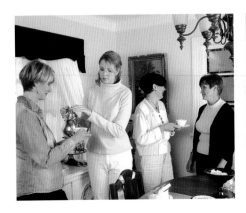
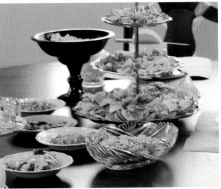
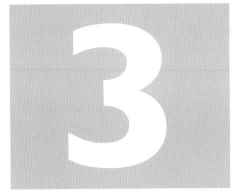
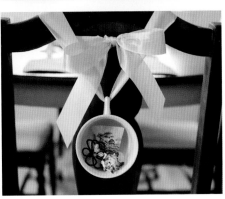
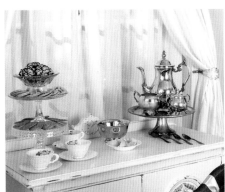

Smashing Tea Party

I HAVE FOUND that many people are intimidated and stand-offish at the prospect of breaking dishes and doing a project. However, most adapt very quickly and slip right into a mosaic mind-set. I decided it would be fun to throw a party instead of holding a class in order to share my love and knowledge of mosaics with some of my good friends. I chose a tea party for my theme and built my party around it.

China cups and saucers automatically evoke the tea party theme. Our party was called a "smashing tea." Of course, I already had plenty of supplies, materials, and equipment on hand, and for my project bases I chose papier-mâché boxes that are easily found at craft stores. I spent most of my planning time finding interesting focus pieces that would

OPPOSITE: *These papier-mâché boxes were created by four women who were not experienced mosaic artists. Each piece is unique and impressive.*

ABOVE: *I invited only four guests to my tea party because of space limitations. With the decorations and table settings, I tried to provide a relaxed and intimate setting to inspire creativity.*

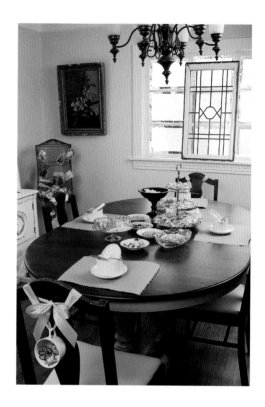

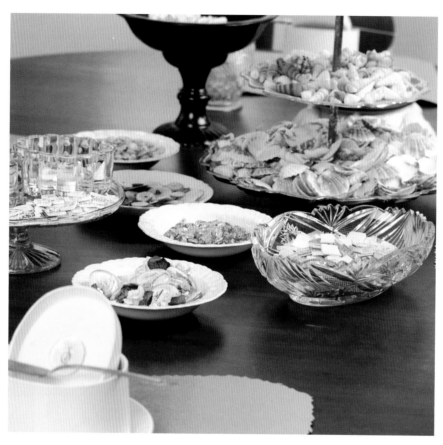

suit the personality of each guest. I used my dining-room table as our work area and a side buffet for food service. Deciding on the food was not difficult; I served tea and cookies.

Because ours was a tea party, I arranged appropriate, project-sized materials in dishes and serving pieces that would normally hold scones, savories, and sweets. The materials table looked as good as the dessert buffet. Each place setting had brown wrapping paper for a place mat, an ironstone saucer for mastic and paint, and a silver butter knife for spreading mastic. I glued flat, clear marbles with the guests' initials onto the inside of the box lids and stood the lids up in the boxes to serve as place cards. I assembled the inspiration collections in cups, which were tied to the backs of the chairs with silver ribbon.

Everyone had the same base, but each inspiration collection was made up of different found objects and chipped china pieces. This provided them with a color scheme and focal

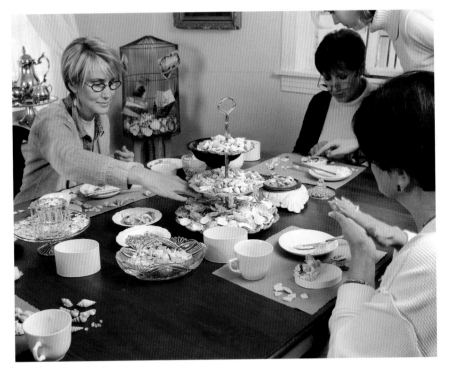

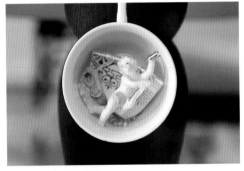

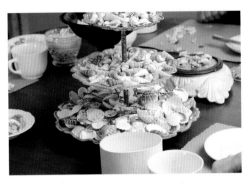

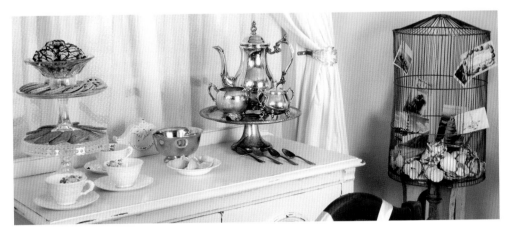

ABOVE LEFT & ABOVE RIGHT:
In a well-thought-out party, all the details of putting the mosaic together have been taken care of—make certain to take the time to precut the china and arrange shells and found objects so they are at arm's length.

LEFT: *Having the buffet table nearby, complete with refreshments, helps remind the guests that they are attendees at a party instead of a class.*

point with which to begin their project. The rest of the design was up to them. None of the guests at my tea party were experienced mosaic artists. Yet each one turned out a one-of-a-kind, very impressive project. The finished pieces were stunning and varied from the whimsical to the dramatic.

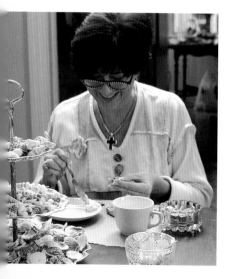
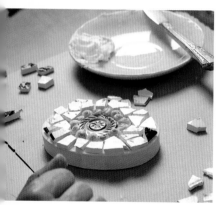
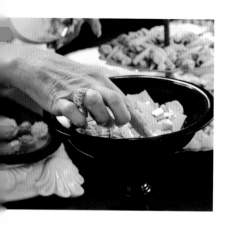
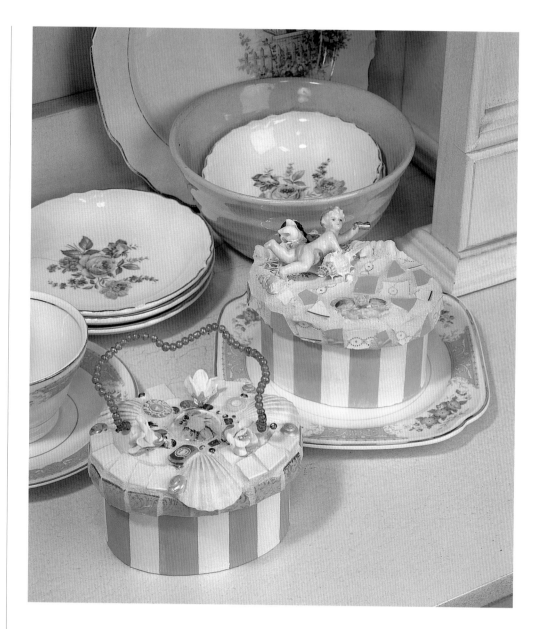

In the end, my guests were thrilled with their boxes, and the party was a "smashing" success. They had a wonderful time, and all of them said they would love to create another project and could not wait to host their own party. The only problem was vanity—the women began to bicker and quibble over whose project was the prettiest!

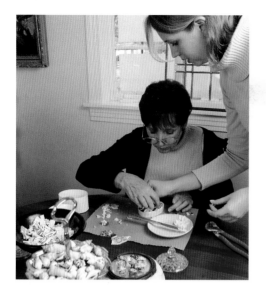

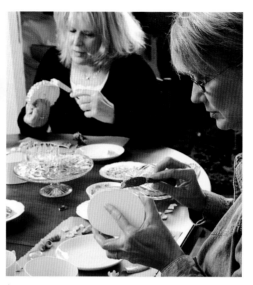

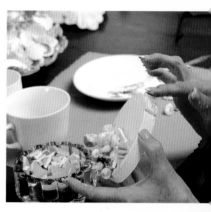

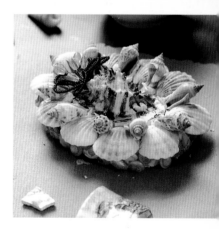

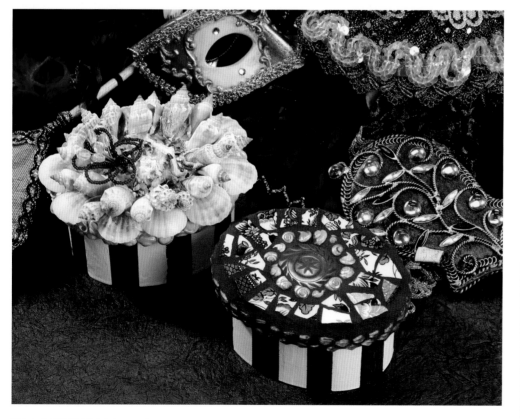

ABOVE & OPPOSITE: *Creating a mosaic in a collaborative setting can be a very rewarding experience. As the host, you should be prepared to spend your time helping your guests complete their projects.*

LEFT & OPPOSITE: *Shown are the completed masterpieces.*

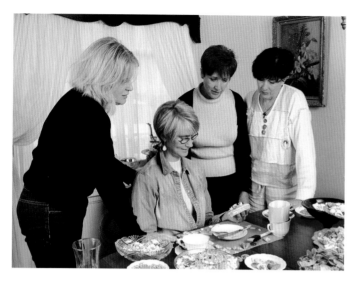 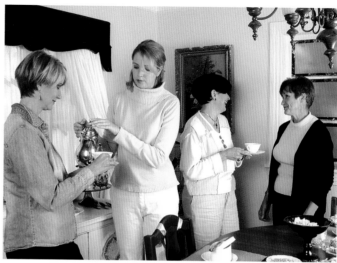

ABOVE LEFT & ABOVE RIGHT:
*Once the process of making
mosaics is complete, take time to
enjoy the refreshments and the
company of good friends.*

When the guests were finished with their projects, we took the time to enjoy a cup of tea and more good conversation.

THROWING YOUR OWN MOSAIC PARTY

If you would like to host your own afternoon of making mosaics, you may find the following lists helpful for putting it all together. You do not have to repeat what I have done—make the party your own by choosing your own theme, refreshments, and project. Remember to provide a fun and relaxed atmosphere that inspires creativity. You and your guests are certain to find a mosaic party to be a rich and rewarding time spent together.

PLANNING YOUR PARTY

- Decide on the party theme and scope
- Choose a project or projects
- Collect supplies, materials, and equipment
- Arrange two separate entertainment areas
    1. For a project work area
    2. For refreshments
- Decide on the food to be served

INVITING GUESTS

- Decide on a manageable number of guests to invite
- Choose people who will enjoy the project and each other
- Choose a date and time that will be convenient for your guests
- Contact guest by regular mail, e-mail, or telephone
- Tell guest to wear comfortable work clothes and plan about three hours for the party

SETTING UP

- Precut china into project-sized pieces
- Arrange the shards and other objects in containers to fit the party theme
- Compile an inspiration collection for each guest
- Layout workstations with gloves, spreader, mastic dish, and inspiration collection
- Mark each workstation with a place card
- Collect a pile of necessary items: tape, wet wipes, paper towels, tile nippers, etc.
- Provide creative music

CHOOSING A THEME

Birthday party—Supply the materials and each guest can make their own party favors.

B.Y.O.P.—"Bring Your Own Project" parties allow people to use their own collected or cherished items in a project.

Fund-raiser—A booth set up where people pay for small bags of shards and then apply them onto a table or piece of furniture would make a great fund-raiser for an organization, and be a fun and unusual attraction. The project could then be raffled or auctioned.

Garden party—A garden party could be held outside, where guests could create projects like stepping stones, flowerpots, or birdbaths.

Holiday ornament party—Shell and mosaic items make wonderful Christmas ornaments. Together, a group could make enough to cover an entire Christmas tree.

"Quilting" party—Like the old-fashioned quilting bee where women came together to work on one project, having several women do a table or one piece of furniture would make for an interesting project and a fun party. The project could then be donated or sold.

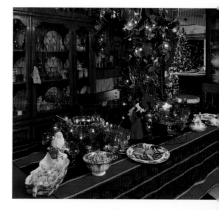

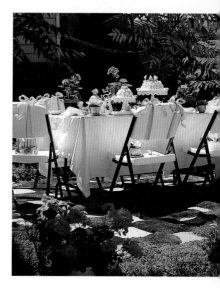

ABOVE: *Choose a theme for your party that suits your purpose. Build the selection of mosaic materials, decorations for the work area, and refreshments around this theme.*

ABOUT THE AUTHOR

Elizabeth DuVal, shown here with her cat, Stinky, is a self-trained mosaics artist who has mastered picasiette and shellwork techniques. Her first project was a footstool that she patterned after one she saw on a TV home design program. Now, more than five years later, she enjoys creating mosaics of both large and small scale, wherein she incorporates shells and intricate patterns that are inspired by vintage dishes.

FROM THE AUTHOR

When I was first asked to write this book I was a little taken aback to be honest. Me? They want me to write a book? They must think I know what I'm doing.

Like most untrained artists, I'm always a bit shy about speaking with authority. I have not been formally trained, so what do I have to offer that is worthy of you reading? As I was fretting over whether or not to write this book, a friend reminded me that through trial and error, I have gleaned a tremendous amount of information. She wisely pointed out that I have accumulated five years worth of knowledge. She said, "Liz, your experience is equivalent to a college degree." She had a good point. I do have a lot to offer! I am in a position to help you avoid the disastrous mistakes I have made.

Through this book, it has become my mission to help you avoid buying plates that will not break, cutting yourself on sharp broken edges, and destroying days of work in the final stages of grouting. It has also been my delight to design and create projects that I sincerely hope will inspire you to become as obsessed as I am with picasiette, shard art, and shellwork.

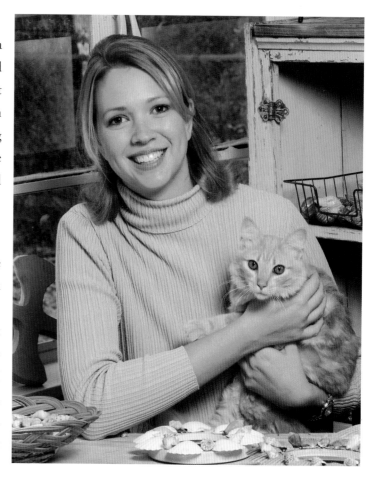

ACKNOWLEDGEMENTS

Special thanks go to Freddy Alvarado, Virginia Barrett, Karen Dawkins, Nicole DuVal, Rhonda Hunt, Kathy Johnston, Janet Noblet, Ashu Meherali Punjani, Raul Romero, Sue Sanderson, Diane Smith, David Sollohub, Jennifer Spak, Barbara Stoessner, and Laura Towery.

DEDICATION

For my mother, Anne DuVal, who had the foresight to believe in me even when I didn't believe in myself.

METRIC EQUIVALENCY CHARTS

mm-millimetres   cm-centimetres
inches to millimetres and centimetres

inches	mm	cm	inches	cm	inches	cm
⅛	3	0.3	9	22.9	30	76.2
¼	6	0.6	10	25.4	31	78.7
⅜	10	1.0	11	27.9	32	81.3
½	13	1.3	12	30.5	33	83.8
⅝	16	1.6	13	33.0	34	86.4
¾	19	1.9	14	35.6	35	88.9
⅞	22	2.2	15	38.1	36	91.4
1	25	2.5	16	40.6	37	94.0
1¼	32	3.2	17	43.2	38	96.5
1½	38	3.8	18	45.7	39	99.1
1¾	44	4.4	19	48.3	40	101.6
2	51	5.1	20	50.8	41	104.1
2½	64	6.4	21	53.3	42	106.7
3	76	7.6	22	55.9	43	109.2
3½	89	8.9	23	58.4	44	111.8
4	102	10.2	24	61.0	45	114.3
4½	114	11.4	25	63.5	46	116.8
5	127	12.7	26	66.0	47	119.4
6	152	15.2	27	68.6	48	121.9
7	178	17.8	28	71.1	49	124.5
8	203	20.3	29	73.7	50	127.0

yards to metres

yards	metres	yards	metres	yards	metres	yards	metres	yards	metres
⅛	0.11	2⅛	1.94	4⅛	3.77	6⅛	5.60	8⅛	7.43
¼	0.23	2¼	2.06	4¼	3.89	6¼	5.72	8¼	7.54
⅜	0.34	2⅜	2.17	4⅜	4.00	6⅜	5.83	8⅜	7.66
½	0.46	2½	2.29	4½	4.11	6½	5.94	8½	7.77
⅝	0.57	2⅝	2.40	4⅝	4.23	6⅝	6.06	8⅝	7.89
¾	0.69	2¾	2.51	4¾	4.34	6¾	6.17	8¾	8.00
⅞	0.80	2⅞	2.63	4⅞	4.46	6⅞	6.29	8⅞	8.12
1	0.91	3	2.74	5	4.57	7	6.40	9	8.23
1⅛	1.03	3⅛	2.86	5⅛	4.69	7⅛	6.52	9⅛	8.34
1¼	1.14	3¼	2.97	5¼	4.80	7¼	6.63	9¼	8.46
1⅜	1.26	3⅜	3.09	5⅜	4.91	7⅜	6.74	9⅜	8.57
1½	1.37	3½	3.20	5½	5.03	7½	6.86	9½	8.69
1⅝	1.49	3⅝	3.31	5⅝	5.14	7⅝	6.97	9⅝	8.80
1¾	1.60	3¾	3.43	5¾	5.26	7¾	7.09	9¾	8.92
1⅞	1.71	3⅞	3.54	5⅞	5.37	7⅞	7.20	9⅞	9.03
2	1.83	4	3.66	6	5.49	8	7.32	10	9.14

INDEX